CSET
Physical Education Exam
Practice Questions

CSET Test Release dates for Agriculture, Art, Business, Dance, HealthScie...
Home Economics, Industrial & Technology Education, Music,
Physical Education, Preliminary Educational Technology and Theatre.

Testing Window	Test Results Release Day
7/31/2023-8/27/2023	→ 9/15/2023
11/20/2023-12/17/2023	→ 1/5/2024
01/15/2024-2/11/2024	→ 3/1/2024
3/11/2024-4/7/2024	→ 4/26/2024

Exam Date: 8/2/2023
@ 11:00am

DEAR FUTURE EXAM SUCCESS STORY

First of all, **THANK YOU** for purchasing Mometrix study materials!

Second, congratulations! You are one of the few determined test-takers who are committed to doing whatever it takes to excel on your exam. **You have come to the right place.** We developed these practice tests with one goal in mind: to deliver you the best possible approximation of the questions you will see on test day.

Standardized testing is one of the biggest obstacles on your road to success, which only increases the importance of doing well in the high-pressure, high-stakes environment of test day. Your results on this test could have a significant impact on your future, and these practice tests will give you the repetitions you need to build your familiarity and confidence with the test content and format to help you achieve your full potential on test day.

Your success is our success

We would love to hear from you! If you would like to share the story of your exam success or if you have any questions or comments in regard to our products, please contact us at **800-673-8175** or **support@mometrix.com**.

Thanks again for your business and we wish you continued success!

Sincerely,
The Mometrix Test Preparation Team

TABLE OF CONTENTS

Practice Test #1

Practice Questions

TABLE OF CONTENTS

Practice Test

Subtest I: Growth, Motor Development, and Motor Learning; The Science of Human Movement

1. During practice, John made all of his free throws. During the game, John missed all of his free throws. Which type of constraints likely impacted John's performance negatively?
   a. Individual and functional constraints
   b. Individual and environmental constraints
   c. Individual and task constraints
   d. Individual and biological constraints

2. Which of the following accurately describes the cardiovascular activity recommendations for elementary-aged children?
   a. An accumulation of 30 minutes every day
   b. 30 minutes of continuous activity every day
   c. An accumulation of 60 minutes every day
   d. 60 minutes of continuous activity every day

3. Which of the following PE activities demonstrates motor or movement skills that a typically developing student should be able to perform by the end of the third grade?
   a. Using a bat to hit a ball pitched by another → by the end of the third grade.
   b. Catch, dribble, pass ball to moving partner → by the end of fourth grade.
   c. Jumping a rope while others are twirling it → by the end of kindergarten.
   d. Jumping a rope that one is twirling oneself → by the end of second grade.

4. Which of the following best contrasts perceptual motor abilities and physical proficiency abilities?
   a. Muscular endurance and muscular strength
   b. Reaction time and control precision
   c. Reaction time and muscular strength
   d. Control precision and finger dexterity

5. In which of the following school levels is movement education most appropriate?
   a. Pre-kindergarten
   b. Elementary school
   c. Middle school
   d. High school

6. Which of these is true about characteristics of developmentally appropriate physical education?
   a. Children are more different individually than they are alike.
   b. Children go through all of the same stages of development.
   c. Children go through developmental stages in varying order.
   d. Children as individuals all develop at the same or similar rate.

1

7. When learning new PE skills, students need more _____ feedback; when they have developed more competence and confidence in certain PE skills and can analyze their own performance, they can make better use of _____ feedback.

a. Extrinsic; intrinsic
b. Intrinsic; extrinsic
c. Positive; negative
d. Constructive; corrective

Students need extrinsic or external feedback from teachers when learning new PE skills & when they learn more competence & confidence in PE skills, they can analyze their own performance by the better use of their internal or intrinsic feedback

8. Which of the following statements best describes the impact of verbal feedback compared to nonverbal feedback?

a. Verbal feedback is more effective than nonverbal feedback
b. Verbal feedback is less effective than nonverbal feedback
c. Verbal and nonverbal feedback aid in student learning
d. Nonverbal feedback is the gold standard

tell - show - do (verbal) (visual) (kinesthetic)

Combining verbal, nonverbal & kinesthetic feedback is ideal as these accommodate diverse learners.

9. Regarding feedback that physical education teachers and coaches give students and athletes, which of the following is an example of prescriptive feedback rather than descriptive feedback?

a. "You can do this!"
b. "Follow through!"
c. "That was great!"
d. "Way to play ball!"

Presp Prescriptive feedback = which is specific. It specifies any instruction that corrects or improves what the student is doing. Choice (a) (c) & (d) are descriptive = which is general.

10. Which of the following best describes the recommended delivery types of student feedback in physical education?

a. Verbal, positive
b. Verbal, kinesthetic, positive
c. Kinesthetic, review, kinesthetic
d. Verbal, visual, kinesthetic

*Verbal = tell
Visual = show
kinesthetic = do

(tell - show - do) approach ✓*

gives students +ve reinforcement by encouraging & praise but does NOT specify exactly what it was that they did well or need to do better or differently.

11. The teacher consistently provides direct verbal and demonstrative feedback to beginning students. What is the purpose of using these feedback strategies?

a. To diversify feedback delivery
b. To help students practice the desired outcome
c. To help students perfect the desired outcome
d. To help students understand the desired outcome

12. Which of the following best describes the environments for open vs. closed motor skills?

a. a tennis match vs. a basketball game
b. a basketball game vs. a round of golf
c. a round of golf vs. a tennis match
d. a gymnastics routine vs. a tennis match

In open settings, the individual is not in complete control & makes decisions based on teammates (offenses) and opponents (defenses); whereas in a closed motor skill, the individual has complete control when deciding to strike the ball as in golf, tennis, gymnastics etc.

13. According to social learning theorist Albert Bandura, which of the following factors that influence observational learning most involves practicing kinesthetic and neuromuscular patterns repeatedly to imitate the teacher or other model's demonstration?

a. Attention → *meaning student must observe teacher modeling.*
b. Retention → *students must encode & store movements patterns in memory for retrieval.*
c. Reproduction → *students repeatedly practice kinesthetic & neuromuscular patterns model-until they can imitate them.*
d. Reinforcement → *which motivates students to perform well.*

14. Prenatal, infant, and child motor development progresses from the head down. This is known as:

a. Cephalocaudal development
b. Proximodistal development
c. Mediolateral development
d. Intellectual development

Cephalocaudal literally means "head to tail." → development ferns inside out

→ like cognitive development & doesn't refer to patterns of motor or physical development.

15. Which of the following best illustrates recommended warm-up and cooldown protocols for secondary students?

a. Ballistic warm-up and static cooldown
b. Static warm-up and dynamic cooldown
c. Dynamic warm-up and static cooldown
d. Dynamic warm-up and ballistic cooldown

Static stretching is recommended to elementary students because they are still learning how to move and control their bodies.

16. Which of the following is a kinesthetic skill improvement technique used in physical education?

a. the sandwich method
b. knowledge of results
c. video analysis
d. knowledge of feedback

* Video analysis along w/ verbal feedback is most effective in improving kinesthetic skills

17. Regarding perceptual-motor abilities, which is a performance skill that would be MOST affected by individual differences in control precision?

a. Playing quarterback in football
b. Handling a hockey puck
c. Dribbling a basketball
d. Driving a race car

18. Ms. Paul notices that many girls never have the ball in possession long enough to develop ball-handling skills during team sports games. What strategy can provide girls with opportunities to develop ball-handling skills?

a. Stop teaching team sports activities
b. Add a rule that girls must touch the ball at least once before scoring
c. Practice ball-handling skills in isolation
d. Allow girls to play amongst themselves

Skill isolation is appropriate when developing or learning a new skill.

[handwritten note: Early adolescents → 20 minutes bou High school students or older aldo → 20-60 minutes bouts every day]

19. Which of the following is considered a best practice for continuous aerobic training bouts for elementary-aged students?

a. 60-minute bouts
b. 45-minute bouts
c. 30-minute bouts
d. 15-minute bouts

[handwritten note: 60 minutes every day moderate-vigorous physical activities are recommended from K-12 students; however, students in elementer should engage 15 minutes bouts of continu activity several times a day to accumulate the 60 minute recommendation.]

20. Which of the following best describes the purpose of teaching chasing, fleeing, and dodging games?

a. To prepare students for invasion games
b. To develop effort and spatial awareness
c. To teach locomotor movements
d. To teach non-locomotor movements

[handwritten note: Spatial awareness: relationships w/ self, others, equipment & effort. ex: tennis, basketball]

21. Students are going to run on the track at the hottest point of the day. Which of the following physical or environmental risks should be addressed?

a. Hypermobility
b. Hypothermia
c. Hyperthermia *(over heating)*
d. Hyperemia

[handwritten note: hypo = low   hyper = high]
[handwritten note: hypermobility = joints beyond the normal range hyperemia = too much blood pools one's area which can be during static exercise.]

22. Positive health behaviors include regularly being physically active, getting a good night's sleep, and eating a nutritious diet. However, adolescent health especially realizes the impact of factors influencing these. Which choice accurately represents one such factor?

a. On a typical day, teens get almost 30 percent of their calories from sugars and solid fats.
b. On a typical day, almost 25 percent of teens watch TV recreationally for three hours or more.
c. On a typical day, parental support and sibling activities have no influence on teens.
d. On a typical day, most high school students sleep fewer hours nightly than needed.

23. Among PE activities applying the concept of effort qualities, which type primarily applies the mechanical principle of time?

a. Having students use their bodies to create impetus moving them through space
b. Having students apply specified movement patterns as fast and slow as they can
c. Having students utilize paddles to propel balls to make them bounce off of walls
d. Having students practice jumping over different objects having different heights

[handwritten note: (a) (c) and (d) applies mechanical principle of force]

24. Divers and skaters can control the speed of their turns through the length of the rotation radius around the center of gravity. Relative to this biomechanical principle, which choice is true?

a. The body turns less slowly with arms extended.
b. The body turns most slowly in the pike position.
c. The body turns most slowly in full tuck position.
d. The body turns most slowly in lay-out position.

[handwritten note: The body will turn fastest w/ the smallest radius-of rotation and body will turn slowest w/ greatest radius of rotation. Extended arm creates longest radius, so body turns slow.]

4

25. One of the skill cues for landing after a jump are bent or "soft" knees. Which of the following best describes the purpose of this skill cue?
   a. To land with the feet parallel
   b. To land with the feet shoulder distance apart
   c. To land to absorb the body's weight
   d. To land to recover faster for the next jump

26. A fifth-grade class is scheduled immediately after a first-grade class. What is the best management system to ensure a safe transition of equipment?
   a. End class 10 minutes early for setup and breakdown
   b. Alternate between first grade and fifth grade for equipment management
   c. Train students to breakdown and set up equipment
   d. Use the same equipment for both groups

27. Lisa engages in aerobic activities three times a week for 30-minutes. Which of the following fitness management principles is Lisa engaging in?
   a. frequency, time, and type
   b. intensity over time
   c. fitness maintenance over time
   d. cardiovascular maintenance over time

FITT Frequency Intensity Time & Type

28. Some athletes engage in altitude training prior to endurance running events. Which of the following is a physiological benefit of altitude training?
   a. An increase in exercise recovery
   b. A decrease in blood flow
   c. An increase in blood flow
   d. A decrease in stress hormones

29. A student-athlete took his body mass index (BMI) and is concerned that he is in the overweight category. Which of the following body composition measurements may be more suitable for this student?
   a. skinfold measurements → inexpensive accurate measure of body fat.
   b. hydrostatic weighing
   c. the Bod Pod — expensive & it measures of body fat
   d. waist circumference measurement — is a measure used to predict cardiovascular risk.

30. Heart disease is the number one killer in the United States. Which activities have the greatest impact on reducing heart disease risks?
   a. Jogging, swimming, cycling — Aerobic exercises
   b. Body weight training
   c. Circuit training
   d. Anaerobic training

31. Which of the following are the movement pathways used to teach locomotor movements?
   a. straight, curved, zigzag
   b. right, left, forward, diagonal
   c. straight, forward, backward
   d. zigzag, forward, backward

32. Regarding safety for young children, which statement is most appropriate?

    a. Parents must teach young children to avoid poisonous products and electrical outlets instead of using storage and safety covers.

    b. Parents must keep young children away from hot appliances and strap them into car seats rather than teaching them such things.

    c. Parents should not let young children explore, as their curiosity and confidence exceed their experience and judgment.

    d. Parents' undergoing physical stress and emotional stress is responsible for the majority of the injuries that young children sustain.

33. Cardiovascular endurance training in hot environments can cause heat illnesses. Which of these is the most severe kind?

    a. Heat exhaustion

    b. Heat cramps

    c. Dehydration

    d. Heat stroke

34. Which of the following cardiovascular and endurance training risk-reduction steps can be used in physical education programs?

    a. A PAR-Q

    b. A talk test

    c. A medical waiver

    d. A warm-up

35. Which of the following is a risk of engaging in cardiovascular endurance training in the cold?

    a. hypothermia

    b. hyperthermia

    c. vasodilation

    d. getting a cold

36. Which of the following should be part of the risk management plan?

    a. Notifying the school counselor

    b. Notifying parents or guardians

    c. Taking attendance

    d. First aid and CPR certification

37. Typical safety guidelines for ascending climbing ropes in portable or permanent installations on school or commercial sites are best reflected by which choice?

    a. A working phone is only needed for installations outside of the school.

    b. An accessible first aid kit is unnecessary at installations within schools.

    c. All climbing ropes are compatible with all activities, plus belay devices.

    d. Equipment must meet standards and be made for the planned activity.

38. Which of the following is a benefit of progressive partner-resistance exercises?

    a. Less isolation of the muscle trained

    b. Safer on the muscle trained

    c. Promotes understanding of the muscle trained

    d. Equipment is not required for the muscle trained

39. Max fell forward when performing an isometric squat. Which of the following biomechanical factors contributed to this forward motion?

    a.   the heels are flat
    b.   the chest is too low
    c.   the feet are too wide
    d.   the hips are not far back enough

40. Among the major body systems, which types of muscles produce voluntary movement?

    a.   Skeletal muscles
    b.   Smooth muscles
    c.   Both these types
    d.   Neither of these

Subtest II: The Sociology and Psychology of Human Movement; Movement Concepts and Forms; Assessment and Evaluation of Principles

1. Which of the following is an objective method for students to self-assess their physical activity levels over time?
   a. using calorie counters
   b. writing journal entries
   c. using heart rate monitors
   d. writing reflections

2. Which self-assessment methods have shown to foster students' interest in improving their fitness?
   a. Health-related fitness testing
   b. Skill-related fitness testing
   c. Comparing fitness results with peers
   d. Tracking progress in journals and fitness logs

3. Which of the following is the purpose of assessment in physical education programs?
   a. To assess teacher effectiveness
   b. To assess lesson plans
   c. To measure learning
   d. To measure objectives

4. Which of the following is the best reason for a self-assessment assignment?"
   a. To refine skills
   b. To assess learning preference
   c. To aid the teacher in the summative assessment
   d. To practice the summative assessment

5. The teacher is concerned that he talks too much during instruction, which reduces student engagement. How can the teacher assess if his concerns are accurate to determine if changes should be made?
   a. Ask another PE teacher for instructional feedback
   b. Ask the principal to conduct an informal observation
   c. Employ an Academic Learning Time assessment
   d. Have students assess instructional delivery

6. Some schools and students do not have certain technologies like heart rate monitors and accelerometers to measure aerobic intensity. What alternative methods can be used to monitor aerobic exercise intensity?
   a. Count steps or track distance covered
   b. Talk tests or rate of perceived exertion
   c. Ask a peer to monitor intensity or sweat production
   d. Cardiopulmonary resuscitation or dry mouth

7. Which of the following strategies is helpful in reducing student conflict?

    a. Modeling expected behaviors
    b. Using peer mediation
    c. Separating the students with conflict
    d. Calling the parents

8. During individual sports, the player does not have teammates to rely on. What attribute helps individual sport athletes perform well?

    a. Positive transfer from team sports
    b. Coach and parental support
    c. Resilience
    d. Self-efficacy

9. Which of the following best describes the purpose of rhythmic activities?

    a. To learn music tempo
    b. To learn how to perform
    c. To learn how to control the body
    d. To learn the locomotor movements

10. Which of the following strategies is recommended when selecting weight training activities for beginning students?

    a. Utilizing dumbbells
    b. Utilizing bodyweight
    c. Utilizing a one-repetition max strength test
    d. Alternating light and heavy weight

11. Among manipulative skills used in sports, which of these does NOT use the hands?

    a. Dribbling as in basketball
    b. Trapping as in soccer
    c. Throwing in general
    d. Catching in general

12. Which technique aids in the refinement and integration of locomotor skills?

    a. Utilizing demonstrations
    b. Incorporating movement concepts
    c. Leading and following
    d. Isolation of locomotor skills

13. Which of the following best describes the order of periodization used for sports conditioning?

    a. Transition, preparation, competition
    b. Preparation, competition, transition
    c. Competition, transition, preparation
    d. Preparation, transition, competition

14. Ari's tennis ball lands beyond the baseline (out of bounds or long) during her tennis forehand. What strategy will help Ari keep the ball in-bound?

    a. Adding topspin
    b. Reducing the power at the point of contact
    c. Increasing the speed of the racket
    d. Bringing the striking arm closer to the body

15. For a student who has joint problems but wants to be physically active, which is the best extracurricular activity?

    a. Skiing
    b. Swimming
    c. Skateboarding
    d. Playing soccer

16. Which of the following is a logical sequence to teach the front crawl stroke in swimming?

    a. Floating, treading water, arm stroking, breathing, kicking
    b. Arm stroking, kicking, front crawling, breathing
    c. Breathing, floating, kicking, arm stroking
    d. Doggie paddling, front crawling, breathing

17. Which of the following best describes the motor skills used in basketball, tennis, and floor hockey?

    a. Manipulative skills
    b. Offensive skills
    c. Closed skills
    d. Defensive skills

18. PE teachers must instruct students to monitor their heart rates during and after aerobic exercise. At what time should they instruct students to take their recovery heart rates?

    a. After cooling down
    b. Right after exercise
    c. While cooling down
    d. Between exercising

19. Several students walk with rounded shoulders or hunched backs. Which of the following exercises will foster good posture and flexibility?

    a. curl-ups
    b. back extensions
    c. pectorals deck
    d. lateral raises

20. Peter and Rob are the same age, height, and weight. Peter has a high level of cardiovascular fitness, and Rob does not engage in any physical activities. Which of the following illustrates Peter's physiological responses at rest and during aerobic exercise compared to Rob?

    a. Higher heart rate and greater stroke volume
    b. Lower heart rate and greater stroke volume
    c. Lower heart rate and smaller stroke volume
    d. Higher heart rate and smaller stroke volume

21. Tina does not have time to engage in aerobic exercises for long periods of time for conditioning. Which of the following activities will help Tina gain aerobic fitness with her current schedule?
    a. HIIT training ⟹ *aerobic exercises for long periods*
    b. Fartlek training — *random intervals – designed to increase running speed.*
    c. Plyometric training — *anaerobic (powerful movement training)*
    d. FITT training — *for health related fitness*

22. Which movement concept is the focus of teaching students how to move forward, backward, and on a diagonal?
    a. Spatial awareness
    b. Locomotor awareness
    c. The concepts of effort and force
    d. Awareness of time

23. The overhand throw consists of a wind up, step, rotation, and follow through. Which of the following best describes the fundamental skill category for the overhand throw?
    a. locomotor movement
    b. non-locomotor movement
    c. manipulative movement
    d. weight transfer movement

24. Which of the following is a non-locomotor movement skill?
    a. Skipping
    b. Bending
    c. Walking
    d. Galloping

25. Which dance form is best reflected in the following dance sequence?
    1. Do-si-do
    2. Circle left
    3. Allemande left
    4. Swing
    a. Folk dance
    b. Ethnic dance
    c. Square dance
    d. Modern dance

26. The teacher notices that students have had difficulty getting open in both team handball and basketball. What are effective strategies for getting open?
    a. Pivot and go
    b. Give-and-go
    c. L-cut
    d. Triple threat

11

27. Students in physical education participate in an annual dance-off fundraising competition with students in the dance program. The competition involves several performances which require strength and stamina. In addition to practicing the dance routines for 60 minutes, five days a week, which of the following conditioning protocols should the students utilize?

    a. Aerobic training two days a week
    b. Strength training two days a week
    c. Aerobic training five days a week
    d. Strength training five days a week

28. Which of the following methods best improves high complex skill combinations?

    a. part practice
    b. whole practice
    c. whole-part-whole practice
    d. small-sided games practice

29. Which of the following technique cues aids in correcting an overthrown ball during an overhand throw?

    a. speed – "Increase the speed of the wind-up motion."
    b. release – "Release at 2:00 or 10:00 o'clock."
    c. follow-through – "Buckle your seatbelt."
    d. foot control – "Take a smaller step towards the target."

30. Which of the following is an etiquette practice expected in tennis and golf?

    a. point or stroke loss for infractions
    b. using the same ball throughout the game
    c. silence
    d. retrieving awry balls

31. The teacher is preparing for the invasion games unit in which last year's students struggled with decision-making during game play. Which instructional approach or model is most appropriate to help students with the decision-making process?

    a. Sport Education model
    b. Tactical games approach
    c. Direct teaching approach
    d. Cooperative learning approach

32. Among positive social behaviors that participating in PE activities can foster in students, learning to take turns in PE classes generalizes to other classes and to life. This corresponds most closely to which social asset that PE participation promotes?

    a. Cooperation
    b. Leadership
    c. Teamwork
    d. Friendship

33. Which of the following activities aids in the development of respect and leadership?

    a. Gymnastics
    b. Team sports
    c. Individual sports
    d. Dance

34. Which of the following helps students build confidence to perform a skill?

    a. Skill cues
    b. Competitive activities
    c. Watching others
    d. Self-talk

35. Which of the following modes of representation did Jerome Bruner describe as emerging the earliest in child cognitive development?

    a. Iconic representation →b/w ages 1 & 6
    b. Enactive representation → infancy
    c. Symbolic representation → ages 7 & up
    d. They all develop simultaneously

36. Which of the following is an example of a psychological approach that aims to develop intrinsic student motivation in physical education?

    a. Self-determination theory → psychological approach
    b. Behaviorism theory → Psychomotor
    c. Social theory → affective
    d. Constructivism theory → psychomotor & affective

37. According to experienced PE teachers, which of the following is true about classroom management in PE classes for the elementary grades?

    a. Making eye contact is more important than learning student names for rapport.
    b. Post gym rules and consequences clearly and deliver consequences consistently.
    c. Stay on the move constantly throughout class; do not have your back to the wall.
    d. Making positive comments reinforces good behavior but does not encourage it.

38. Some female students avoid weight training exercises for fear of getting very large and looking more masculine. Which of the following is an appropriate response to these students to dispel this myth?

    a. inform them to use bodyweight in lieu of free weights
    b. inform them that it is possible to get stronger without getting bulky
    c. inform them that their nutrition intake would need to greatly increase
    d. partner them with female students who weight train but are not abnormally large

39. Research finds cooperative learning beneficial across school subjects. It is particularly applicable to PE, which involves a high proportion of team and small-group activities. Which component of cooperative learning entails student reflection on group or team progress toward learning goals?

    a. Social skills
    b. Group processing
    c. Individual accountability
    d. Positive interdependence

13

40. Which of the following has been shown to foster lifelong physical activity?
   a. Competence in physical activities
   b. Modeling physical activity
   c. Participating in organized sports
   d. Having active parents

Subtest III: Professional Foundations; Integration of Concepts

1. During the outdoor high school tennis unit, which of the following is an appropriate modification for students who struggle to get the ball over the net during the forehand stroke?

a. Lowering the net
b. Practicing against a wall
c. Getting closer to the net
d. Watching a peer demonstrate the forehand

2. Jennifer, a student with visual impairment, has difficulty seeing the colors on the archery targets. Which type of adaption should the teacher consider?

a. a task-specific adaptation
b. an equipment-specific adaption
c. a boundary-specific adaptation
d. a task and boundary-specific adaptation

3. Which of the following strategies helps accommodate multiple abilities in physical education classes?

a. Teaching to the outcome
b. Providing extensions
c. Employing standards-based instruction
d. Incorporating differentiation

4. Which of the following is a benefit of elective physical education programs?

a. Ensures enough equipment for all students
b. Caters to the teacher's strengths
c. Students decide their program
d. Helps with non-PE course schedules

5. The teacher chooses squad lines to take attendance so she can easily see if students are absent. Which of the following is a limitation to this approach?

a. squad lines are outdated
b. squad lines are teacher-centered
c. squad lines take too much time
d. squad lines can lead to behavioral problems

6. Of the following, which accurately reports research findings related to how physical fitness affects academic achievement?

a. Cardiovascular fitness and body mass index (BMI) correlate positively with test scores in achievement.
b. More physically fit children react more quickly but not necessarily more accurately.
c. Children burn more calories during active gaming than teacher-led fitness activities.
d. Intense exercise is followed by a significant temporary decline in cognitive function.

7. What is true about how teachers can engage community members and groups in physical education (PE) programs?

a. It would be inappropriate to solicit funds from local health agencies to buy sports equipment.
b. Local trophy companies are in business to make money and will not donate for school events.
c. Local governments lack departments that could talk to students about community resources.
d. When PE teachers plan Olympics-themed events, they may find volunteers from local colleges.

8. Adaptation through exercise is a major principle of which of these sciences, which also applies the others?

a. Anatomy
b. Physiology
c. Kinesiology
d. Neurology

9. In one instructional method to promote psychomotor learning, a physical education teacher clearly explains learning goals and skills to be learned to the students; demonstrates the skills for the students; and provides the students with practice time, frequently and regularly monitoring their progress during practice. This describes which of the following methods?

a. The contingency or contract method
b. The command or direct method
c. The task or reciprocal method
d. None of these methods

10. A PE teacher helping high school students set short-term fitness goals for personal fitness plans explains how SMART criteria aid goal setting; e.g., the "S" means Specific: students must identify what they want to accomplish, how, and why it matters to them. Which SMART component most informs whether goals are realistic?

a. The "M"
b. The "R"
c. The "A"
d. The "T"

11. In addition to physical activity, which of the following activities has been shown to help manage stress?

a. Drinking red wine
b. Getting adequate sleep
c. Watching television
d. Drinking caffeine

12. Which of the following is a strategy used for refinement of manipulative skills?

a. tag games
b. increased opportunities to respond
c. leading and following a peer
d. choice of manipulative skill

13. Which of the following movement concepts help facilitate relationships with objects in the environment?

    a. forward and backward
    b. over and under
    c. straight and curved
    d. strong and light

14. Regarding physical, emotional, and social factors that influence personal physical health, which of the following is true?

    a. Anxiety and depression cause sleep and diet problems but not cardiovascular troubles.
    b. Stress and family dysfunction cause emotional problems, not physical illness.
    c. Air pollution can aggravate asthma but is not actually found to cause asthma.
    d. People can overeat and be overweight, and yet still suffer from malnutrition.

15. What have physical education teachers found about using apps like Coach's Eye, iCoachview, and so on with their students?

    a. Student enthusiasm helps them appreciate constructive criticism.
    b. Students typically cannot use apps after only brief demonstration.
    c. Students are uncomfortable seeing their performance postgame.
    d. Students experience delayed feedback when teachers play videos.

16. Which of the following is an example of integrated physical education?

    a. Allowing students to choose curricula that relate to classroom content
    b. Having students analyze the angles of underhand and overhand throws
    c. Inviting specialists to cover topics such as yoga
    d. Inviting classroom teachers to teach concepts

17. Which of the following biomechanics subjects are based on calculus?

    a. Vector composition and resolution
    b. Differentiation and integration
    c. The parallelogram method
    d. None of these topics

18. What is the purpose of using a drum to teach dance?

    a. Better control of the tempo and effort
    b. Provide students with creative alternatives
    c. Allows students to take turns using the drum
    d. Closer alignment to convey the movement concepts

19. Which component of health-related physical fitness is most dependent on the others?

    a. Flexibility/mobility
    b. Body composition
    c. Cardiovascular endurance
    d. Muscular strength

20. Throughout the school year, the teacher randomly teaches dances submitted by students at the beginning of the school year rather than focus solely on the recommended dances, e.g., square dance, in the curriculum. Which of the following concepts is the teacher promoting?

    a. self-efficacy
    b. diversity
    c. choice
    d. autonomy

21. Regarding physical education teacher communication with parents, what is MOST effective related to posting and communicating class rules to students at the beginning of the school year?

    a. Giving rules to students, but not parents, so students feel they can trust teachers
    b. Giving copies of rules to students with instructions to take them home to parents
    c. Sending the rules by postal mail with a cover letter asking parents to review them
    d. E-mailing the rules to the parents with a cover letter asking them to review them

22. Which of the following best illustrates the purpose of physical education?

    a. To develop lifelong learners
    b. To develop athletes
    c. To develop healthy bodies
    d. To develop movement competence

23. Researchers tested a three-year intervention, Physical Activity Across the Curriculum (PAAC), with 4,905 children in elementary schools using a randomized, controlled trial. Which choice do you think most likely describes one of their findings?

    a. Students enjoyed physically active lessons more than teachers did.
    b. More physical activity in schools competed with instructional time.
    c. Bandura's self-efficacy is significant for setting and achieving goals.
    d. PA integration is expensive, and requires replacing the curriculum.

24. Recent trends and philosophies about PE and its role in both encouraging physical activity (PA) and using it to promote positive student development include which of the following?

    a. Children and teens are resources for developing competencies.
    b. Children and teens are problems that adults need to manage.
    c. Physical activity promotes health, not happiness, for Americans.
    d. Only educators can use PA to optimize development for youth.

25. A student trips over her shoelaces and hits her head on the volleyball standards during gameplay. Which of the following should the teacher have done to reduce the risk of liability?

    a. tied the student's shoelaces
    b. nothing as it was an accident
    c. covered the standards with padding
    d. posted the potential risks

26. The principal notices that students with disabilities are sitting on the sidelines during physical education because the teacher indicated it was too difficult to change her plans to meet all students' needs. Which of the following laws of inclusion does the teacher violate?

    a. Individuals with Disabilities Education Act
    b. Individualized Education Program
    c. Adapted Physical Education
    d. Federal Education Records and Privacy Act

27. Among the following common areas of negligence in physical education, in addition to first aid emergencies, which one can teachers and coaches MOST mitigate by enlisting the help of students?

    a. Instruction
    b. Supervision
    c. Transportation
    d. Class environments

28. Title IX regulations regarding gender equity in PE stipulate which of the following?

    a. Student participation in PE classes may be refused or required by gender.
    b. Student participation in PE classes may not be subject to ability grouping.
    c. Student participation in body contact sports may not be separated by sex.
    d. Student participation in PE skills must be assessed by unbiased standards.

29. Which of the following laws gives women and girls equal access to sports and education?

    a. Title IX
    b. Roe v. Wade
    c. Women's Rights Act
    d. The Civil Rights Act

30. Students track and reflect on their successes, failures, and engagement with classmates during the ball handling activities, and rate their performance at the end of class. Which of the following teaching models is evident in these tasks?

    a. Cooperative learning
    b. Guided discovery
    c. SEL
    d. TPSR

31. Regarding communication with athletes, which statement is recommended by experts for coaches to consider?

    a. Coaches must not only get athlete attention but also explain, so athletes understand easily.
    b. Coaches must determine if athletes understood them but not whether they believed them.
    c. Coaches must get athletes to understand and believe, not necessarily accept, what they say.
    d. Coaches must disregard athletes' individual and group nonverbal cues for controlling them.

32. The federal government defines basic elements of furthering student development through physical activity (PA) that PE programs and teachers promote. How are these elements structured to accomplish major PE goals?

a. Attaining participant developmental health outcomes enables creating optimum contexts for PA, which enables providing universal PA opportunities and access.
b. Creating optimum contexts for PA enables providing universal PA opportunities and access, which enables attaining participant developmental health outcomes.
c. Providing universal PA opportunities and access enables creating optimum contexts for PA, which enables attaining participant developmental health outcomes.
d. Attaining participant developmental health outcomes enables providing universal PA opportunities and access, which enables creating optimum contexts for PA.

33. What amount of quality physical education time most reflects the National Association for Sport and Physical Education (NASPE) recommendation for elementary school students?

a. A minimum of 15 minutes per day
b. A maximum of 30 minutes per day
c. A minimum of 30 minutes per day
d. A maximum of 60 minutes a week

34. A first-year teacher has started at a school without a curriculum or lesson plans. Where should the teacher go for resources to help select developmentally appropriate activities for instruction?

a. Contact former physical education teachers
b. Consult state and national guidelines
c. Ask a veteran teacher
d. Ask the principal

35. Which of the following strategies increases instructional time?

a. Preparing equipment ahead of time
b. Observing students looking for fatigue
c. Wearing a watch
d. Adhering to the bell schedule

36. The teacher blows the whistle one time for students to start activities and uses "freeze" to stop activities. Which of the following strategies is the teacher engaging in?

a. instructional cues
b. transition cues
c. focus cues
d. equipment management cues

37. Which of the following best explains the purpose of using instructional models in physical education?

a. To structure activities for learning
b. To complement the standards
c. To meet all students' needs
d. To simplify planning

38. What are the minimum cardiovascular activity recommendations for students in middle school?

    a. 20-minutes a day
    b. 30-minutes a day
    c. 45-minutes a day
    d. 60-minutes a day

39. Coach Wheelock refuses to let the girls on the school's basketball team play with the boys in physical education because he says the boys play too rough. Which of the following practices does Coach Wheelock exhibit?

    a. Safety for injury prevention
    b. Gender discrimination
    c. Favoritism towards the boys
    d. Gender stereotypes

40. A student sprains their ankle in class. Which of the following is an appropriate method to notify the parents or guardians?

    a. Send a note home with the student
    b. Send an email
    c. Call the parent or guardian
    d. File the accident report in the student's records

Answer Key and Explanations

Subtest I: Growth, Motor Development, and Motor Learning; The Science of Human Movement

1. B: Given John's free throw-shooting ability (task constraint), his performance was negatively impacted due to individual and environmental constraints. Individual constraints include structural constraints (e.g., height, body size, gender, and equipment) and functional constraints (cognitive and psychological issues, including arousal). Spectators, fans, and different noises occur during game play, which is a different environment than the practice environment. John is also playing against opponents instead of teammates, which is also an environmental constraint. As such, these environmental constraints are having negative impacts on John's performance.

2. C: The Centers for Disease Control and SHAPE America recommend that elementary-aged students engage in an accumulated 60 minutes of moderate to vigorous cardiovascular activities every day. Young children fatigue faster than older children, and bouts longer than 15-20 minutes are developmentally inappropriate. Activities should include games and activities that keep students moving (e.g., tag) rather than structured exercise programs.

3. A: Typically developing students should be able to hit a ball pitched by another by the end of the third grade. They should be able to demonstrate sport-specific movement skill combinations, e.g., catch, dribble, and pass a basketball to a moving partner (b) by the end of the fourth grade. They should be able to jump a rope twirled by others (c) by the end of kindergarten. They should be able to jump a rope they twirl themselves (d) by the end of the second grade.

4. C: Reaction time is a perceptual motor ability as it uses the senses and is dependent on the environment, such as a starting gun in track or having to play defense. Whereas muscular strength is reliant on physiological factors and less dependent on the environment e.g., a student's coordination or ability to do push-ups.

5. B: Elementary is the most appropriate school level to teach movement education as it is the foundation for the fundamental movements (locomotor and non-locomotor), movement concepts (spatial awareness, relationships, and effort), and the three domains of learning (psychomotor, cognitive, and affective). These foundational skills and concepts aid in progressive, mature movements taught in middle and high school needed for individual and team sports, as well as fitness activities. Some pre-kindergarten programs are included in elementary school physical education programs, while others are offered at daycare centers.

6. B: Characteristics of developmentally appropriate PE include that individual children are more alike than different, not vice versa (a); that individual children all go through the same developmental stages (b); that they go through these stages in the same, not varying, order (c); and that individual children develop at different rates, not all at the same or similar rates (d).

7. A: Students need more extrinsic (external) feedback from teachers or coaches when learning new PE skills. When they are more competent and confident with certain PE skills, they can analyze their own performance and make use of this intrinsic (internal) feedback. Choice (b) has this backwards. Students need both positive feedback for reinforcement and encouragement and negative feedback for correction (c), and both constructive and corrective (d) feedback, at all learning stages.

8. C: Both verbal and nonverbal feedback aid in student learning and are more effective when used together. The effectiveness of each type of feedback is dependent on the learning style of students. For auditory learners, verbal feedback may be more effective, and for visual learners, nonverbal feedback may be best. Combining verbal, nonverbal, and kinesthetic feedback is ideal, as these accommodate diverse learners.

9. B: "Follow through!" is an example of prescriptive feedback, which is specific. It specifies an instruction that corrects or improves what the student or athlete is doing or needs to do. In this example, it tells the student or athlete that, when batting, kicking, throwing, and so on, he or she must follow the movement through for it to be effective rather than stopping it abruptly upon contact or release. The other examples are all descriptive feedback, which is general. It gives students or athletes positive social reinforcement by encouraging or praising their performance in general but does not specify exactly what it was that they did well or need to do better or differently.

10. D: Recommended delivery types of feedback include verbal (tell), visual (show), and kinesthetic (do), also known as tell-show-do. The tell-show-do approach is rooted in social learning theory, which allows students to gain deeper understanding of movement concepts and competence when instructional feedback incorporates these three methods. Multiple modalities allow students to engage all of the senses, create a mental image of the movement shown, and also encourages modeling. All of these have shown to increase skill acquisition and performance, especially when learning a new skill.

11. D: Beginning students make lots of errors and focus heavily on skill cues, so the teacher needs to be intentional and direct with instruction to help the student understand the movements of the skill. As students begin to understand the movement as illustrated in improvement, the need for direct feedback and demonstrations are reduced.

12. B: A basketball game requires open motor skills because the environment is unpredictable. In open settings, the individual is not in complete control and makes decisions based on teammates (offenses) and opponents (defenses). In contrast, golf is a closed motor skill where the individual has complete control when deciding to strike the ball. Tennis takes place in an open-skill environment, but the tennis serve is a closed skill as the server controls the movement. Gymnastics is a closed motor skill environment as the gymnast decides when and how to move and is not reliant on others.

13. C: Bandura identified and described observational learning. Among factors influencing it, he included Attention (a), meaning students must observe the teacher or model; Retention (b), meaning students must encode and store movement patterns in memory for retrieval; Motor Reproduction (c), meaning students repeatedly practice the kinesthetic and neuromuscular patterns modeled until they can imitate them; and Incentives and Reinforcement (d), which motivate students to perform the others.

14. A: Cephalocaudal means literally head-to-tail. This is the pattern of physical development for human embryos, fetuses, infants, and children. Proximodistal (B) means development from the inside out, which is also a pattern of human physical growth. (These two are not mutually exclusive but concurrent.) Mediolateral (C) is not a term generally used; but *medial* means toward the midline or closer to the inside, and *lateral* means away from the midline or closer to the outside, so "mediolateral" would have a meaning similar to proximodistal. Intellectual development (D) is like cognitive development and does not refer to patterns of motor or physical development.

15. C: A <u>dynamic warm-up involves low-intensity aerobic activities and mobility exercises to prepare the body for the demands of m</u>ore intense activities by getting blood flow to the muscles that will be used during the activity. A static cooldown helps return the body back to normal and increase flexibility by holding the stretch for longer periods of time. Static stretching is recommended for elementary-aged students because they are still learning how to move and control their bodies. Ballistic stretching or bouncing should be avoided because they increase the likelihood of overstretching or muscle tears.

16. C: Video analysis allows for continued review of kinesthetic skills where the performer can see what they did well and what needs improvement. Video analysis along with verbal feedback has shown the most effective in improving kinesthetic skills. The sandwich method is a feedback delivery method that sandwiches corrective or critical feedback with positive feedback. The type of corrective feedback given will determine if it is useful. The knowledge of results is terminal feedback that provides input on the outcome, whereas knowledge performance feedback positively impacts motor skills. Knowledge of feedback is awareness of the feedback provided—no matter the type.

17. B: Handling a hockey puck is an example of a performance skill that would be affected most by individual differences in the perceptual-motor ability of control precision. Football quarterbacking (A) is an example of a performance skill that would be affected most by individual differences in the perceptual-motor abilities of response orientation or choice reaction time. Dribbling a basketball (C) is an example of a performance skill that would be affected most by individual differences in the perceptual-motor ability of manual dexterity. Driving a race car (D) is an example of a performance skill that would be affected most by individual differences in the perceptual-motor ability of rate control.

18. C: Skill isolation is appropriate when learning or developing a new skill. Practicing skills in isolation slows down the pace. As skills gradually improve, the challenge should increase, like incorporating speed, a defender, and engaging in small-sided games. While most physical education programs are coed, research shows that girls engage in more physical activity and are more skillful in same-gender PE programs; however, isolation of skills would still occur in same-gendered classes. A "touch" will likely not lead to proficiency in ball-handling skills because the opportunities to develop are limited.

19. D: Sixty minutes every day is the recommended amount of moderate to vigorous physical activity for all K-12 students; however, it is recommended that students in elementary grades engage in 15-minute bouts of continuous activities several times a day to accumulate the 60-minute recommendation. Early adolescents are encouraged to engage in at least 20-minute bouts. Older adolescents or high school-aged students are encouraged to engage in continuous physical activity from 20- to 60-minute bouts each day.

20. B: Chasing, fleeing, and dodging games help develop the movement concepts of spatial awareness, relationships with self/others/equipment, and effort. These movements also help with strategies and tactics used in individual (tennis) and team sports (basketball).

21. C: The teacher needs to address student risks of hyperthermia or overheating, which increases when engaging in physical activities in the heat. The teacher needs to account for dehydration, which increases the risks of heat exhaustion, heat cramps, and heatstroke and can lead to death. Hydrating, resting frequently, wearing protective barriers such as sunscreen and hats, and adhering to the school's temperature guidelines are all excellent ways to avoid heat-related health issues. Hypothermia is when the body's temperature drops significantly below normal and occurs when in cold conditions such as cold air or cold water, for extended periods of time. Hypermobility is when the joints go beyond the normal range of motion. Hyperemia is when too much blood pools to one area, which can increase during static exercises.

22. D: According to the US Department of Health and Human Services (HHS) Office of Adolescent Health (OAH), on typical days teenagers get almost 40 percent of their calories from sugars and solid fats, not 30 percent (a); recreational TV watching equals or exceeds three hours for almost one-third of teens, not one-quarter (b); parental support and active siblings DO influence adolescents to become and remain active (c); and the majority of teens sleep fewer hours nightly than needed for good health (d).

23. B: Having students apply specified movement patterns, which have been timed in advance, as fast and as slowly as they can, applies the mechanical principle of time. Choices (a), (c), and (d) are all PE activities that apply the mechanical principle of force. (Another movement effort quality applies the mechanical principle of balance.)

24. D: The body will turn slowest with the greatest radius of rotation, and fastest with the smallest rotation radius. Extending the arms creates the longest radius; therefore, the body turns *more* slowly, not less, with arms extended (a). In the pike position, the body turns at a medium speed (b); pulling the arms in toward the body shortens the radius, causing faster rotation. So the body turns fastest in full tuck position (c), and slowest in lay-out position (d).

25. C: Bent or "soft" knees help the body absorb the force of the body's weight during the jump. Keeping the legs straight increases the risk of musculoskeletal injuries. Keeping the feet parallel and shoulder distance apart will help the jumper maintain balance during the landing, and the rest time between jumps aids in recovery.

26. C: Students should be trained to breakdown and set up equipment to speed up transition time. Ending class 10 minutes early is inappropriate because students lose instructional/learning time. Using the same equipment is likely developmentally inappropriate, given the size and strength differences between first and fifth grade, and the content taught should be different. Alternating between groups is likely to cause confusion and disrupt routines, which increases classroom management.

27. A: Lisa is engaging in an exercise frequency of 3 days a week, time of 30-minutes each session, and running for type of exercise, which are three components of the FITT Principle. Lisa's intensity of exercise is the unknown component of the FITT principle. It appears that Lisa is engaging in activities that may put her in the cardiovascular maintenance stage, but there is not enough information to make this determination. If she were engaging in this same level of activity for months, one could conclude that Lisa is engaging in cardiovascular maintenance, since she is not increasing or decreasing in her exercise levels, though we cannot determine her overall fitness with these indicators.

28. C: Altitude training is beneficial because there is an increase in blood flow to the muscles and oxygen transport, which increases aerobic capacity and reduces fatigue; however, there are also risks, which include slower rates of exercise recovery and an increase in stress hormones (e.g., cortisol).

29. A: Skinfold measures are more suitable for this student-athlete as it is an inexpensive accurate measure of body fatness. BMI is an estimate based on height and weight and does not take muscular weight into account causing false overweight or obesity assessments. Hydrostatic weight and the Bod Pod are superior methods of measuring body fat but are expensive and not practical in a physical education or high school setting. Waist circumference is an easy measure that is used to predict cardiovascular risk, but it does not estimate or predict levels of excessive body fat.

30. A: Aerobic activities including jogging, swimming, and cycling have shown to have the greatest impact on reducing heart disease risks. Engaging regularly in these activities increases blood flow through the arteries, reduces blood pressure, and helps with maintaining a healthy body weight. Body weight training is a type of resistance training using the body. While body weight exercises can include aerobic activities (e.g., jumping jacks), results are not as impactful as jogging, swimming, and cycling unless done using a high-intensity interval training (HIIT) format. Circuit training has similar outcomes as bodyweight training and has benefits to heart health by moving from exercise to exercise, but aerobic activities are specific to training the cardiovascular system.

31. A: The pathways used to teach locomotor movements are straight, curved, and zigzag. Moving right, left, forward, backward and diagonal are directions the body can travel and are used to teach locomotor movements, dance, and sports skills.

32. D: Public health research shows most injuries children sustain occur when parents are operating with inadequate sleep and/or nutrition, are overly taxed emotionally, and/or are undergoing relationship difficulties. Because of the danger, parents should not simply try to teach young children to avoid poisonous substances and electrical outlets; they should take home precautions like storing poisons out of children's reach and plugging safety covers into outlets (A). However, in addition to keeping them away from hot appliances and strapping them into car seats, parents should also teach young children not to touch stovetops, ovens, toasters, etc., and always to sit in their car seats (B) to attain balance among allowing children's exploration, supervising them as much as possible, and teaching them fundamental safety precautions and rules. Although it is true that young children develop independence, curiosity, and confidence before gaining experience and learning good judgment, their exploration within reason is a normal, healthy, and important developmental process that parents should not inhibit (C).

33. D: The mildest form of heat illness is dehydration (c), caused by fluid loss through perspiration. Exercising too long in the heat causes greater fluid loss and also salt loss, which can cause heat cramps (b), the next mildest form. If one continues exertion after experiencing dehydration or heat cramp symptoms, this can lead to more serious heat exhaustion (a). Intense exertion in the heat can make the body produce more heat than it can release, resulting in heat stroke (d), the most severe form.

34. A: Although student health risks are generally shared with physical education teachers from school personnel, administering a Physical Activity Readiness Questionnaire (PAR-Q) is a simple proactive measure to identify potential health risks associated with cardiovascular and endurance training. A PAR-Q asks students/participants/parents to respond to health history questions that may negatively impact activity such as a history of asthma or musculoskeletal injuries. Athletics and sports programs require physicals for participation, but they are generally not required in physical education programs. A proper warm-up reduces the risk of injury as it prepares the body for vigorous activity when engaging in cardiovascular activities. However, a warm-up does not identify potential health risks. A talk test is a self-evaluation of exercise intensity.

35. A: Hypothermia is a condition when there is a considerable drop in body temperature resulting from exposure to extreme cold conditions or prolonged exposure in cold environments. Exposure to cold water increases hypothermia risk. Hyperthermia is a condition when there is a significant increase from exposure to heat or prolonged physical activity in hot environments. Vasodilation increases blood flow and sweat response to cool the body while training in warm and hot temperatures. Vasoconstriction occurs to decrease blood flow to keep the body warm or reduce heat loss when training in the cold. Cold weather does not cause colds; germs cause colds, which may occur in hot or cold conditions.

36. D: First aid and CPR certifications are components of risk management plans designed to help teachers prepare, assess, and respond to injuries and illness. Notifying the school counselor or notifying parents or guardians does not minimize risk, but it does inform of risk or an event. Taking attendance is a classroom management strategy to keep a record of students who are present, tardy, or absent.

37. D: PE classes must have a working cell phone or other communication device, regardless whether the equipment installation is in the school or elsewhere (a); the same applies to having a fully stocked, easily accessible first aid kit (b). Climbing ropes must also be compatible with the planned climbing activity and the belay device selected; these are NOT all compatible (c). Equipment must be manufactured specifically for the activity planned, and meet uniform standards (d).

38. D: Progressive partner-resistance exercises (aka partner-assisted manual resistance) allows for better isolation of the muscle trained, as the partner is able to apply to greater resistance or additional overload when weights are not available—a good option for PE programs that have little to no resistance training equipment. Students need to be trained prior to attempting this exercise because it is a type of training that can increase the risk of injury. Communication is critical to inform the partner when there is too much resistance applied and when more resistance is required.

39. D: Max's hips are not far back enough during his squat, causing him to lose balance or stability. The heels should be flat as squatting on the toes can also create a forward motion. At one time, deep squats below 90 degrees were frowned upon, but new research indicates that a deep squat performed correctly is safe and does not impact balance. Max is likely to fall back if the chest is too low, which puts more weight in the rear, thus pulling him backward. A lifted chest with the hips back counters this effect.

40. A: The skeletal muscles in the body produce voluntary movement. The smooth muscles (b) are used by the blood vessels and organs like the heart, bladder, etc., to produce involuntary movement. Therefore, both (c) and (d) are incorrect.

Subtest II: The Sociology and Psychology of Human Movement; Movement Concepts and Forms; Assessment and Evaluation of Principles

1. C: Heart rate monitors are tools used to monitor heart rate and cardiovascular fitness intensity, which students can use and track over time. Having a low resting, exercise, and recovery heart rate suggest a good level of cardiovascular fitness. A lower resting, exercise, and recovery heart rate over time suggests improvement in cardiovascular fitness. Students can also use pedometers or step counters to track their steps with a widely accepted health goal of 10,000 steps a day. An increase in step count over time suggests an improvement in activity, but it cannot definitively determine fitness level. Calorie counters track the number of calories consumed for weight loss, maintenance, or weight gain, but they are not a fitness measure. Journal entries and reflections allow students to describe their experiences, including how they feel, e.g., "I am no longer out of breath when I walk up a flight of stairs," but are not objective tools to assess fitness levels.

2. D: When students track progress in journals and fitness logs, they are able to control and visually see progress, which has shown to motivate students to improve fitness levels. Fitness testing can foster student interest, but many students dislike fitness testing. Fitness testing can be harmful and demotivate some students. Fitness testing alone has not shown to improve fitness, only measure it. Students should only focus on their own results and not compare them with peers because the purpose is to improve personal fitness.

3. C: The purpose of assessment in physical education is to measure student learning. If learning is not measured, the teacher will not know their students' level of education or what they are capable of. Teachers reflect on lesson plans to ensure that activities are working towards the objectives, thus fostering learning. Objectives are the outcomes or desired goals, but the assessment is done to measure the learning of the objectives.

4. A: Self-assessment is a self-regulation tool designed to help students evaluate skill development and refine skills. Self-assessment allows students to ascertain the quality of their own performance based on skill cues. They focus on the missed cues to refine the performance. The teacher usually administers a survey or inventory of learning preferences, which helps to plan for instruction. Self-assessment is designed for student growth and should not determine student outcomes because that is the teacher's job. The teacher also administers or determines which summative assessment will be used to establish what was learned.

5. C: While having others observe and provide feedback can be beneficial to improve instruction, teachers should have effective tools that they can implement to assess their own effectiveness. The teacher should employ an Academic Learning Time in PE (ALT-PE) assessment to document the time that he talks during instruction. The teacher can conduct this during class or record the lesson and review the amount of time used talking later. It is inappropriate to ask students to assess a teacher's instructional delivery, as students are there to learn and are not qualified to make such an assessment.

6. B: Talk tests or rates of perceived exertion are methods that can be used for all ages, but are especially recommended when technology is not available and for elementary-aged students because young children have difficulty taking a pulse. Intensity cannot be measured by looking at someone or someone's sweat production because these vary according to body size, fluid intake, and the number of sweat glands. Counting steps or distance only indicates the amount of surface area covered.

7. A: Modeling expected behaviors is a strategy that reduces student conflict. Students often engage in behaviors they see rather than the ones they told are correct. Peer mediation is a strategy used to solve student conflict after it has already occurred. Separating students might be a temporary measure used as a cooling-off period but is also implemented after the conflict. Furthermore, cooperation and working with others are fundamental objectives in most physical education programs, and separating students is not an appropriate long-term solution. Calling the parents is an informative response to conflict that has already transpired but is unnecessary to conduct before any potential conflict.

8. D: Self-efficacy is the personal belief of accomplishment in motor skills and performance. As players become more competent in skill and game performance, their self-efficacy tends to increase. The player has to be able to self-motivate and coach themselves to be successful in individual sports because there is no one to depend on during a poor performance. While grit and resilience can help players persevere through difficult experiences, a person with these attributes can still lack self-efficacy in performance (e.g., 0-6 loss in tennis to a less skilled player).

9. C: Rhythmic activities like dance and creative movements help students learn to control their bodies. While music is often used, the primary goal is body control. Locomotor, non-locomotor, and manipulative movements are used during rhythmic activities which can aid in the performance of skills, like gymnastics or dance routines.

10. B: Bodyweight exercises are recommended for beginning students in weight training. Bodyweight exercises reduce the risk of injury and teach students how to move the body for physiological adaptations. After bodyweight exercises, light weights, including dumbbells, are introduced with gradual increases in weight. Students are often directed to select a light weight and perform a few reps and, if too easy, select a heavier weight in small increments until the last two or three reps in an 8-to-15-rep count are challenging. This can be used to conduct a predicted one-repetition max test by using predicted one-rep max calculators. The one-repetition max strength test is not appropriate for physical education as lifting the heaviest amount possible in one-rep increases injury risk. Alternating between light and heavy weight is a training method for muscular strength and endurance goals but is not employed with beginners.

11. B: Dribbling in basketball (a) is bouncing a ball, typically down to the floor using the hands. Throwing (c) uses one or both arms and hands to project a ball or other object away from the body into the air. Even throwing using equipment, as in jai alai, requires hands. Catching (d) stops a moving object's momentum using the hands. Trapping in soccer (b), however, uses the feet or other body parts, but NOT the hands, to control or receive the ball.

12. B: The movement concepts of spatial awareness, relationships, and effort help refine and integrate skills, as combining these elements increases the locomotor movements' challenge, thus fostering mature movement patterns needed for manipulative activities. Demonstrations, as well as leading and following, aid in the refinement of the basic locomotor movements but will not independently help the student achieve skill integration and refine higher-level skills without incorporating the movement concepts.

13. A: Transition, preparation, and competition are the three phases of periodization used for sports conditioning. The transition, or post-season, phase is when athletes recover and maintain fitness levels through cross-training. During pre-season, the preparation phase is where skill and sport-specific fitness is developed to prepare for the competition phase, where athletes maintain fitness and work on areas for competitive play.

14. A: Ari can help keep the ball inbounds by adding topspin, which will cause the ball to drop downward instead of going out of bounds. This is achieved by moving the striking arm from low to high with follow-through over the opposite shoulder. Increasing the speed of the racket may result in the ball traveling farther out. Stroke technique and contact point are more impactful than the amount of power placed on the ball.

15. B: Of the activities named, swimming is ideal for students with joint problems because it puts no weight or stress on the joints. The buoyancy of the body in water keeps weight and impact off the joints. Students can be active and get exercise without aggravating joint conditions or pain. Skiing (A) requires a lot of knee bending and turning, hip swiveling, and bearing weight on the joints, so it is not compatible with joint problems. Skateboarding (C) also involves much knee bending and turning, as well as jumping and landing, and would be hard on joint problems. Playing soccer (D) requires running and kicking, again putting too much impact on the joints. These other sports also are done on the ground and subject to gravity, whereas swimming relieves the joints of weight.

16. A: Floating and treading water are generally taught first because they are water safety and survival skills that require less energy and help build confidence for swimming. Floating and treading water also teach beginner swimmers about the buoyancy of their bodies. The arm motion tends to come next, followed by breathing and arm strokes while standing before putting all the steps together with the flutter kick. Sometimes breathing is taught last because it is widely accepted as the most difficult part of the front crawl stroke (aka freestyle). When breathing is taught last, the order or introduction of arms and kicks do not matter.

17. A: While offensive and defensive skills are evident in basketball, tennis, and floor hockey, manipulative skills best describe the use of motor skills, which encompasses offensive and defensive movements. Manipulative skills are advanced fundamental movement skills that combine locomotor and non-locomotor skills and include fine and gross muscle movements while using equipment. Skills performed in team and dual sports are open skills, as the environment is unpredictable.

18. A: Recovery heart rate should be taken by feeling the pulse for 15 seconds after cooling down, 5-6 minutes after the last aerobic exercise. It should not be taken before cooling down (b), during cooldown (c), or in between exercises (d). Recovery heart rate should be 120 beats per minute (bpm) or lower for safeness and effectiveness; if higher, the next workouts' intensity should be lowered.

19. B: Back extensions will help with posture by increasing flexibility in the lower back, which causes the shoulders to pull back to an upright position. Kyphosis is an age-related hunched back condition that generally occurs in older women and differs from the hunched back postures among some students. Curl-ups may further the rounded or hunched back posture. A counter-balance exercise including push-ups would aid in posture corrections. The pec deck may also aid in the rounding of shoulders and back. A counter-balance exercise including rear delts would help with posture.

20. B: Regular engagement in aerobic activities aids in cardiovascular fitness. Physiological adaptations that occur include a lower resting heart rate, both at rest and during exercise, and a greater stroke volume. The heart becomes stronger as a result of cardiovascular fitness and is able to force or pump blood (stroke volume) throughout the body with less effort.

21. A: Tina can engage in high-intensity interval training (HIIT), which is as effective as long bouts of aerobic or endurance activities to improve cardiorespiratory fitness. Fartlek training consists of random intervals, e.g., run, sprint, recover, repeat, which are designed to increase running speed. Plyometric training is a powerful, explosive, sports-specific movement training, such as rebound jumping in basketball, or jumping for a volleyball spike, which is more anaerobic than aerobic. Frequency, Intensity, Time, and Type (FITT) is the general fitness principle used to guide the health-related fitness components.

22. A: Spatial awareness includes directional movements (right, left, forward, back, diagonal) that inform students of where the body can move. Students can demonstrate directions with locomotor and non-locomotor movements, such as twisting to the right. Effort and force are the intensity of a movement. Time is the rate or speed (fast, slow) of a given movement or activity.

23. C: The overhand throw is a manipulative movement skill that combines non-locomotor or locomotor movement with an object or equipment. Locomotor movements are traveling movements that get a person from point A to point B. Non-locomotor movements are movements without traveling. While weight transfer is done during the overhand throw, weight transfer is a movement concept and not a fundamental skill category.

24. B: Unlike locomotor movements that consist of traveling from one place to another, non-locomotor movements are stationary movements that include bending, stretching, leaning, balancing, twisting, reaching, pulling, and turning.

25. C: Do-si-dos, circles left and right, allemandes left and right, swings, and promenades are dance moves associated with square dance, which are yelled out by a caller. Square dance is performed with four couples that make up a set where dancers may dance with another partner or with one or more groups within the set. Folk dance also has couples, but the couples tend to only dance with each other. Folk dances mark occasions like births, weddings, and other special events. Ethnic dances are associated with a group's ethnic background—some of these are folk dances while others are not. Modern dance consists of a wide variety of movements from various dance forms (ballet, jazz, hip-hop) performed to music that influences or helps create dance sequences. Modern dance is often performed in school programs and dance troupes.

26. C: The L-cut is an effective strategy for getting open, which usually involves a fake/feint towards the defender prior. The triple threat and the pivot occur when a player has possession of the ball, and is used to see the available options (pass, shoot, or dribble). The give-and-go involves one player passing to another player and then immediately cutting toward the goal to receive a pass back from that other player and finally shooting the ball.

27. B: To initiate a physiological response to strength training, students should engage in two to three days of strength training specific to dance needs every week using progressive overload. The repetition in the dance performances will maintain or increase stamina and aerobic fitness. Aerobic fitness may be achieved by practicing the dance routine 60 minutes, five days a week.

28. A: Part practice, or the breaking down of a complex skill like a volleyball spike, has shown to be the most effective method for improving high complex skill combinations. Whole practice or fully completing the skill is best for low complex skills such as running. The whole-part-whole method is ideal for tactical concepts like offense and defense used in team sports where players play the game first. During gameplay, weaknesses are identified, broken down in parts, and practiced before resuming gameplay. Small-sided games allow students to put skills into practice, but mastery of complex skills is unlikely to occur, as the game's pace is too fast; thus, the skill needs to be broken down at a slower rate.

29. C: The angle of release is the issue when a ball is overthrown. Right-handed throwers should release the ball at the 2:00 o'clock position in front of the thrower. Left-handed throwers should release the ball at the 10:00 o'clock position in front of the thrower. The speed of the wind-up does not impact an overthrown ball. The follow-through will put more speed on the ball and is at a diagonal across the body. Taking a step, in opposition towards the target, generates more power in the throw.

30. D: An etiquette practice in golf and tennis is to retrieve any ball that goes awry. Silence is an expected etiquette practice during a serve in tennis and during the stroke in golf, but once the ball is struck, lands, or after a point is earned, it is acceptable for the crowd and spectators to cheer. It is a rule, not a matter of etiquette, for players to use the same ball in golf and balls in tennis unless the balls get lost or damaged. Another rule or penalty in tennis and golf is to lose a point or stroke for infractions.

Copyright © Mometrix Media. You have been licensed one copy of this document for personal use only. Any other reproduction or redistribution is strictly prohibited. All rights reserved. This content is provided for test preparation purposes only and does not imply an endorsement by Mometrix of any particular political, scientific, or religious point of view.

31. B: The tactical games approach (aka Teaching Games for Understanding, or TGfU) is a model designed to teach students situational awareness, or how to make decisions during game play. This approach allows for students to play the game first, then work backwards to solve problems for common situations or errors. Students develop a collection of options to choose from when confronted with certain situations. For instance, when an offensive player has the ball during an invasion game and is doubled-teamed, they pull from the database of effective options rather than freezing up and not knowing how to respond. The teacher tries encouraging students to problem solve rather than tell them the answers as is done during the direct teaching approach. Decisions are made in the Sport Education model, but restricted to the role of the student (coach, scorekeeper, equipment manager) but not specifically to game play. Cooperative learning is embedded in the tactical games approach as students work collaboratively to make team decisions.

32. A: The President's Council on Physical Fitness and Sport reports social assets promoted by PE participation, including skills for leading others (b), working together toward a common goal (c), developing closer, higher-quality friendships (d), and cooperating with others (a), which most closely corresponds to learning to take turns in PE classes, hence in other classes and in life.

33. B: Respect and leadership are skills developed through team sports as students work together to accomplish a goal. Everyone has a role in team sports, including positions played, team captains, cheerleaders, scorekeepers, and referees to demonstrate leadership in their own way. Communication amongst teammates is needed to reach team goals and fosters respect—it takes all involved to express thoughts and listen to each other for the team's greater good. Etiquette and sportsmanship skills are taught and should include respectful engagement with opponents. Someone good at gymnastics may garner respect, but the activity does not lend itself to various roles as it is an individual sport. As with gymnastics, other individual sports foster self-awareness, and reliance, but other than engaging with an opponent, the opportunities to develop respect and leadership are limited.

34. C: Watching other classmates perform a skill helps students build confidence. Skill cues help with the understanding of how to perform a skill, but independently, do not build confidence. Many students are not competitive, and competition has shown to hinder confidence for novice learners. Positive self-talk may help build confidence, but negative self-talk hinders confidence and skill performance.

35. B: Bruner described enactive representation (muscle memory retention of motor response information) as emerging during infancy. Iconic representation (information based on visual imagery) is said to emerge between one and six years of age. At around seven years and older is when he describes the onset of symbolic representation (encoded storage of information via symbols). Since he described these as developing sequentially and not simultaneously, "enactive representation" is the correct answer.

36. A: The self-determination theory is a psychological approach used to teach physical education to increase intrinsic student motivation by providing students with achievable but challenging tasks. Intrinsic motivation has shown most effective in fostering appreciation and lifelong physical activity engagement. Behaviorism focuses on the psychomotor domain and is a teacher-directed approach that works to change students' behaviors based on the environment the teacher creates. Social theory relies heavily on the affective domain, or the social aspects of student engagement, and underpins cooperative and sport education models where students work together to solve problems. Constructivism theory focuses on the cognitive domain and works toward providing students with an understanding of what they are doing and why in the psychomotor and affective domains.

37. B: Experienced elementary PE teachers advise new teachers to establish rapport with students by learning all their names as soon as possible AND making eye contact (a); establish rules and consequences for breaking them, post these in the gym or classroom, review them periodically as a reminder, and always deliver consequences consistently (b) to keep order; BOTH keep moving during class AND teach with backs to the wall (c) to eliminate blind spots and keep an eye on all students; and make positive comments, both to reinforce students following rules AND encourage students who are not to do so (d).

38. B: Female students can get stronger but will not achieve increased muscle mass on their own since the female body produces smaller amounts of testosterone, the dominant male hormone responsible for building and increasing muscle mass. Adolescent males will also have difficulty increasing muscle mass because physiological adaptations of size tend to occur after puberty ceases. Bodyweight exercises are good options when free weights are not available and both are utilized to increase muscular fitness, but without a significant amount of testosterone or growth hormone, female students are not likely to develop large muscles. Free weights are also appropriate for women and girls. A significant increase in nutrient intake can lead to fat weight gain but an increase in nutrient intake alone will not aid in increased musculature. Partnering students with similar goals may be beneficial but this partnership will not likely dispel the myth that female students will look more masculine if they participate in weight training.

39. B: Among cooperative learning components, social skills (a) are incorporated such that students can identify their purposes and applications. Group processing (b) entails student reflection on how well the group or team functioned to work toward its learning goals. Individual accountability (c) involves all individual student members taking responsibility for group or team success, hence being accountable for it. Positive interdependence (d) entails student group work or teamwork in assigned member roles to attain shared goals.

40. A: Competence in physical activities has shown to lead to lifelong physical activity engagement. Modeling is a strategy that can aid in learning how to perform physical activities and build confidence to attempt a movement or skill, but modeling alone has not shown to foster lifelong physical activity. Participating in organized sports can develop competence in specific sports skills, but participation does not equate to competence. Active parents can be role models, but competence needs to be developed to engage in lifelong physical activity.

Subtest III: Professional Foundations; Integration of Concepts

1. C: Getting closer to the net is an appropriate modification as it only requires the student to adjust rather than lowering the nets, which is a difficult, time-consuming task. The student can start closer to the net and take steps back after success to get comfortable with the motion until they can get the ball over the net from farther distances. During gameplay, balls are returned from every court area, which makes this modification more realistic for gameplay. Lowering the net may alter or develop poor technique when returning to the standard net height. Practicing against a wall can aid in stroke development but is not specific to getting the ball over the net. Watching a peer can improve performance, but it is not a modification.

2. B: An equipment-specific adaptation or modification would be helpful and might consist of using bright colors which should be easier for the student with vision impairment to see. The task remains the same, but the object or equipment is adjusted or modified to meet the student's needs. A task-specific adaptation would change the task itself by moving the student closer to the target; however, the student can shoot the arrow; therefore, the task would not change. The boundaries would remain the same as the student's only issue is seeing the colors on the archery targets.

3. D: Differentiation is a strategy that addresses multiple abilities that exist in one class. The teacher should have activities for beginner, intermediate, and advanced students to meet all learners' needs and include extensions and remediations. Some students have mastered or exceeded the learning outcome but still need to be challenged and learn new ways of doing things.

4. C: Elective physical education programs allow students to decide or choose the type of programming. Student choice has been shown to increase student motivation. More focus on students' strengths rather than the teacher's strengths is also a benefit. Equipment is dependent on a budget, but some elective programs might be driven by equipment availability. Equipment, however, should not guide the curriculum or course offerings. Physical education is a part of a holistic educational experience, and the goal is to develop students, not provide scheduling relief.

5. D: Students can get bored sitting in squad lines which increases off-task behaviors or behavioral problems. An active squad line approach and frequently changing squad lines may keep students engaged and lessen boredom and off-task behaviors. Locating absent students is generally a faster approach than taking attendance for all present students. Squad lines are considered vintage or an outdated approach but can be effective for extremely large class sizes and combined with learning outcomes, e.g., active warm-up. Squad-lines may or may not be teacher-centered, which depends on how the squads are created and whether squad line leaders are used. Using squad leaders is a recommendation to speed up taking attendance, provide student-leadership, and reduce boredom.

6. A: Large-scale state research has found that student cardiovascular fitness achievement and healthy body mass index (BMI) scores correlate positively with student scores on the state academic achievement test of knowledge and skills. Other research has found that children who are more physically fit demonstrate not only quicker reaction times but also more accurate responses (B). Another investigation found that children burn more calories and take nearly twice as many steps during teacher-led fitness activities as during active gaming, not vice versa (C). Other studies show that intense exercise is followed by improvement in cognitive function (D).

7. D: When physical education (PE) teachers want to hold events with Olympics themes for students, their local colleges are good places for them to find students willing to volunteer their time and work to help. PE teachers whose schools are short on funds for sports equipment can solicit financial assistance from local health and wellness agencies, which is not inappropriate (A) as these organizations may be able and often want to help. PE teachers also can ask local trophy companies to donate some of their products—and even refreshments as well—to student athletic events; these businesses frequently welcome the good public relations and advertising they can get by helping out schools (B). Local governments do have a department where PE teachers can recruit representatives to present to students about the use of community resources (C): their county and city Parks and Recreation Departments.

8. C: Anatomy (a) is the study of body structures, physiology (b) the study of body functions. Neurology (d) is the study of the nervous system, including the brain. Kinesiology (c) is the study of body movement, functions, and performance; it applies these other sciences. A major principle of kinesiology is adaptation through exercise.

9. B: This is a description of the command or direct method, which uses teacher-centered task instruction to promote psychomotor learning. The contingency or contract method (A) is a behavioral approach that uses specified rewards that are contingent on student task completion to reinforce psychomotor behaviors. The task or reciprocal method (C) uses stations whereby student learning of specific psychomotor tasks is integrated into the learning setup. Because (B) is correct, (D) is incorrect.

10. C: SMART = Specific, Measurable, Achievable, Relevant, Timely. "M" (a) entails identifying numbers, events, or dates for measuring attainments. "R" (b) means goals should matter to the students, and results should affect their lives. "A" (c) means goals, though challenging, should be attainable, not impossible. This most informs whether goals are realistic. "T" (d) means a time element should be included to keep students on track, e.g., the date when they should reach a short-term goal.

11. B: Getting adequate sleep has been shown to help manage stress as it restores and calms the body and improves concentration, decision-making, and judgment. Most sleep recommendations are 8-10 hours a night. Short naps have also been shown to have similar benefits, including strengthening the immune system and regulating blood pressure that increases during stressful events. Watching television can aid in escaping stress, but it can have an adverse effect and increase stress depending on what is viewed and the length of screen time. Drinking caffeine has been shown to increase the stress response and interfere with sleep quality. Drinking one glass of red wine has shown stress reduction benefits, but over indulgence of alcohol interferes with sleep quality and duration. Over indulgence of alcohol can also lead to alcohol dependence and alcoholism.

12. B: Adequate opportunities to respond (OTR) or practicing skills regularly aid in skill refinement. Tag games keep students physically active and help teach movement concepts including speed, dodging, fleeing, and chasing. Leading and following are strategies that aid in the refinement of locomotor skills. Choice is a strategy used to foster motivation to participate.

13. B: The teacher is facilitating relationships with objects by moving over and under equipment. Forward and backward reinforce spatial awareness directions. Straight and curved support spatial awareness pathways, and strong and light are effort or force movement concepts.

14. D: Malnutrition is not only caused by eating too little; it is also caused by eating foods that are not nutritious, eating unbalanced diets, and not getting enough of all necessary nutrients. Thus, people can eat too much and become overweight, but if most of the calories they consume are "empty", i.e., they contain few or no vitamins, minerals, protein, healthy fats, or fiber, they can suffer malnutrition. In fact, overconsumption of refined carbohydrates that lack fiber instead of whole grains; saturated and trans fats instead of monounsaturated and polyunsaturated fats; and processed foods instead of fruits and vegetables contribute to both obesity and malnutrition. Anxiety, depression, and other emotional factors can not only disrupt sleeping and eating, but also cause high blood pressure and heart disease (A). Stress and family dysfunction can cause both emotional and physical illness (B). Air pollution is found both to aggravate and to cause asthma (C).

15. A: Physical education (PE) teachers find that their students are enthusiastic about apps that allow them to view their and classmates or teammates' athletic performance. This enthusiasm makes it easier for teachers to create positive learning environments wherein students are more appreciative of constructive criticism and more motivated to improve their performance. PE teachers find that, after only a brief demonstration, students can easily use them (B) for recording one another, viewing the recordings, and giving each other feedback. Teachers find student athletes really enjoy watching their performance postgame (C) in the locker room. They can much more easily identify which strategies and tactics they used were most and least effective through this viewing. Also, when PE teachers use apps to record video and they play it back, students get much more immediate feedback (D).

16. B: Having students analyze angles of underhand and overhand throws is an example of integrated physical education or cross-curriculum approaches, as the angles of release are a physics concept but taught in a physical education environment. Commonly, schools adopt school-wide initiatives to include cross-curriculum activities to garner a deeper understanding of content. Another teacher teaching non-physical education content is cross-curricular instruction but not integrated within the physical education context. Specialists provide expert training in physical education activities. Student choice does not guarantee integration, and choices tend to be from PE curricula.

17. B: Differentiation is a calculus technique for finding a quantity's rate of change, used in biomechanics to get derivatives of curves or functions like velocity, acceleration, and jerk, which are derivatives of displacement. Integration is a calculus technique to determine the area between an x-axis and a curve, used in biomechanics to obtain integrals like velocity as an integral of acceleration, displacement as an integral of velocity, and work as an integral of power. Composition and resolution of vectors (A) in biomechanics are ways of combining coplanar and concurrent vector quantities by using vector algebra, not calculus. The parallelogram method (C) is a method for resolving vectors in different directions in biomechanics that is based on geometry, not calculus: The parallelogram is a geometric shape. Because (B) is correct, (D) is incorrect.

18. A: Hand drums are used to easily control the tempo and effort which are then used to teach movement concepts. It is easy to strike the drum hard and soft to illustrate effort, or fast and slow to illustrate tempo variation, before moving on to music with a set tempo. The tempo of striking the drum can be dramatically slower or faster than music can provide without the technology to alter music tempo.

19. B: Body composition is the individual body's ratio of lean body mass to body fat. It depends most on the other four components, i.e., flexibility (a), cardiovascular endurance (c), muscular strength (d), and muscular endurance, because improving these will naturally improve the body composition after consistent fitness conditioning over time.

20. B: The teacher is promoting diversity among students as the students' dance preferences are influenced by the students' cultures. Since the students submitted dances at the beginning of the school year, this is not an example of choice. Choice would indicate that the students choose the dance for the day or week, but in this scenario, the teacher is randomly choosing from student submissions. Self-efficacy is the belief that one can perform a skill or task. Autonomy is the freedom and independence to make choices on one's behalf. An example of autonomy in physical education is the freedom to move and choose activities as illustrated in creative movement activities, including dance.

21. D: It is not a good idea to keep class rules from parents in a misguided attempt to gain student trust (A). Parents need to be informed of the rules, so they know what is expected of their children and can make sure their children understand the rules. Teachers also protect themselves by informing parents of rules in advance: In the event of student behavior problems, injuries, or disputes, parents cannot subsequently deny knowledge or accuse teachers of not informing them. Giving the students copies of the rules to take home to parents (B) often means the parents never receive them. Postal mail (C) is much slower when today's technology enables almost instant transmission of e-mails (D), eliminating the potential for events to occur before parents receive the information.

22. D: The purpose of physical education is to develop physical literacy, which is the confidence and competence to engage in a variety of movements or physical activities along with a value and appreciation of physical activity. A healthy body can result from engaging in physical activities, but that is not the main purpose of physical education. Athletic skills can be developed in physical education, but they are byproducts of the overall purpose of physical education. The development of life-long learning is often a broad goal of education, but competence in each educational discipline is often the main purpose.

23. C: According to goal-setting theorists, individuals high in Bandura's concept of self-efficacy (belief in one's own ability to perform a specific behavior successfully) set higher goals, are more committed to goals, and identify and apply better strategies for achieving them. The researchers (Gibson et al., 2008) found teachers and students enjoyed physically active lessons equally (a). By modifying existing content lessons to integrate PA, it did NOT compete with instructional time (b). The PAAC intervention needed no curriculum change and little school cost (d).

24. A: A recent trend emerging among policymakers and educators is the positive youth development perspective. This philosophy regards children and teens NOT as problems adults must manage (b) but resources for developing new or improved competencies (a). The US Department of Health and Human Services (HHS, 2008) published *Physical Activity Guidelines for Americans,* its cover stating the message, "Be active, healthy, and happy!" (c). The President's Council on Physical Fitness and Sports (2009) recommended that parents and healthcare providers, as well as educators, optimize youth development through PA (d).

25. C: The teacher should make sure that the standards were covered with padding to reduce the risk of liability as it is a foreseeable risk. It is not the teacher's responsibility to tie a student's shoes, but if the teacher notices that a student's shoelaces are untied, she should inform the student to tie them or tie them if the student does not know how. The student tripping over the shoelaces was an accident, but if the standards are uncovered, the teacher may be held liable for an injury. Safety rules rather than potential risks should be posted.

26. A: The teacher is violating the Individuals with Disabilities Education Act (IDEA), which guarantees students with disabilities a quality education. Students with disabilities should be engaged in the lesson and instruction given for learning. Physical education teachers should modify activities so that students with physical or mental disabilities can meet the objectives, which is Adapted Physical Education (APE). The Individualized Education Program is a legally binding plan created by a team of professionals (counselors, school psychologists) with parent and teacher input on strategies that help students succeed, like extended time on assessments, read-aloud tests, and taking notes on a computer. The Federal Education Records and Privacy Act protects student records. Consent is required if records are disclosed.

27. B: Physical education (PE) instructors can address negligence in instruction (A) by ensuring they teach students the correct procedures and protocols for safety and for equipment setup, use, and takedown and ensuring students understand and practice how to execute sport and movement activities beforehand. Because PE classes often are large and getting larger, they can address negligence best in supervision (B) by ensuring they continually and actively supervise students throughout all activities and enlisting students to practice peer supervision in addition to supplement teacher supervision. In transportation (C), teachers and coaches are liable outside of school and must obtain written parental consent; follow all school policies, practices, and procedures; and supervise student behavior on buses. In class environments (D), teachers and coaches must be alert for possible dangerous conditions, which can vary daily, and space students to limit hazards.

28. D: Title IX (1972) prohibits sex discrimination in education, including athletics. It stipulates that PE classes may NOT be separate on the basis of gender (a); that students MAY be grouped by ability (b); that students MAY be separated by sex for sports requiring body contact (c), e.g., wrestling, football, boxing, ice hockey, rugby, etc.; and if PE skills are measured using a single standard that affects one sex adversely, another or other standard(s) without gender bias must be substituted (d).

29. A: Title IX gives women and girls equal access to sport and education. Roe v. Wade is the Supreme Court case that gave women the legal right to an abortion, subsequently overturned in 2022. The Civil Rights Act is a law that prohibits discrimination based on race, color, religion, or country of origin in schools, employment, and public spaces. The Women's Rights Act is a civil rights act that protects women from discrimination based on gender, which was not included in the Civil Rights Act.

30. D: The Teaching Personal and Social Responsibility (TPSR) helps students navigate the positives and negatives in life in physical education settings, including success, failure, challenge, and perseverance, that aid in the development of self-evaluation and monitoring. TPSR is designed to teach personal and social skills and help students manage their behaviors in and out of school. Cooperative learning requires students to work together to solve a problem independently of the teacher. Guided-discovery is a type of cooperative learning where the teacher guides students by posing questions or prompts that help them meet the objective. Social Emotional Learning (SEL) focuses on the affective domain and is designed to ensure a safe and equitable environment for all students.

31. A: Experts advise coaches that they must first determine whether they have athletes' attention before communicating with them successfully, and second, whether they are explaining in a way that athletes can understand easily. Third, coaches must determine whether the athletes have in fact understood what they said, and fourth, whether the athletes believed what they told them (B). Fifth, coaches must determine whether their athletes have accepted what they told them (C) as well as understanding and believing it. To control a team or group of athletes, coaches also must be sensitive to the nonverbal cues they give (D), while the coaches are talking. These cues communicate whether the athletes are puzzled, confused, disbelieving, bored, resentful, disrespectful, and so on toward a coach and what he or she is saying.

32. C: The President's Council on Physical Fitness and Sports identifies "Fundamental Building Blocks" for using PE to promote positive student development. The structure of these is that giving opportunities and access to PA for all young people enables establishing ideal contexts for engaging in PA, which in turn allows PE educators to help students attain developmental health outcomes.

33. C: National Association for Sport and Physical Education (NASPE) recommends that elementary school students should receive a minimum of 150 minutes per week of quality PE time in schools, meaning that somewhat more than this would not be too much. Thirty minutes per day most reflects the recommendation of 150 minutes per week as school is in session five days per week. A minimum of 15 minutes per day (A) is not enough. A maximum of 30 minutes per day (B) implies that more than this is bad, which does not reflect the NASPE recommendation. A maximum of 60 minutes for an entire week (D) is also far too little: This would break down to only 12 minutes daily, or two 30-minute classes per week, or three 20-minute sessions, four 15-minute sessions, and so on.

34. B: The first-year teacher should consult the state- and national-level physical education guidelines. Each state has a physical education association with physical education guidelines, and SHAPE America provides national physical education guidelines, standards, and recommendations. Unless the principal was a physical education teacher, they are not a content expert. Former or veteran physical education teachers may not be abreast of current guidelines, standards, and best practices.

35. A: Preparing equipment ahead of time increases instructional time. Observing students who look fatigued is a safety measure to ensure students have adequate rest and water breaks. Wearing a watch can help keep the time of activities but alone does not increase instructional time, nor does adhering to the bell schedule.

36. B: The teacher is employing transition cues to start and stop activities and get the students' attention. Transitions are planned and taught. While transition cues aid in instruction, instructional cues are the communications from the teacher to students to help them meet the learning objective. Cues, in general, are designed to get students to focus or pay attention, but the example is specific to transitions. Equipment management cues would consist of the teacher instructing students to gather the equipment, which is direct and explicit.

37. A: Instructional models (TGfU, Sport Ed, cooperative learning) help structure activities for learning. All of the instructional models used in PE are reflected in the national PE standards. No model or standard can meet all students' needs, but teachers can design activities and use strategies to meet the needs of diverse learners. There are formulas and techniques (e.g., bullet points, 5-step planning) that are used to simplify planning, but the models alone are not designed for simplification.

38. D: It is recommended that middle and high school students engage in 60-minutes or more of cardiovascular activities every day. The 60-minutes can be in one session or accumulated throughout the day. Elementary students should also engage in 60-minutes a day but have shorter bouts of 15 to 20 minutes of continuous activity. Adults should engage in 30-minutes or more a day. Although these physical activity recommendations are endorsed by physical education and physical activity governing bodies, 20-minute and 45-minute sessions also positively impact health, and daily activity is encouraged across groups. Shorter sessions can be maximized with higher intensity activities.

39. D: Coach Wheelock is demonstrating low expectations and gender stereotypes of female students despite their role as basketball athletes. He assumes that they would not be able to play with the boys. He also assumes that all boys play rough, which is another gender stereotype. Rules should be in place to ensure safety for all students. As long as the girls can play basketball in class, separating groups by gender would not be considered gender discrimination or favoritism towards the boys.

40. C: A phone call to the parents should be the first method to contact parents of an injury, followed by an email if available. A note should only be sent home if there is no phone number or email account; however, if the parent can be seen face-to-face (e.g., parent or guardian picks up the child from school), the message should be conveyed at that time. All injuries should be documented on an accident report and filed with the proper school authority.

Practice Questions

TABLE OF CONTENTS

Practice Test

Subtest I: Growth, Motor Development, and Motor Learning; The Science of Human Movement

1. Which of the following is an example of how emotional/behavioral factors can affect young children's levels of physical activity and fitness?

    a. A child diagnosed with ADHD is physically so overactive that he becomes exhausted.

    b. A child diagnosed with asthma needs monitoring for breathing problems in exercise.

    c. A child diagnosed with diabetes needs exercise watched and coordinated with diet.

    d. A child diagnosed with disabilities needs adaptive equipment for physical activities.

2. Of the following choices, which one most describes a stage of motor learning associated with the age period of adolescence?

    a. Purposeful movements develop beyond simple reflexes.

    b. Motor patterns of increasing complexity are developing.

    c. Motor patterns gain increasing automaticity and fluidity.

    d. Ability, motivation, and practice influence development.

3. Kenya is having difficulty with balance and coordination skills in the gymnastic routines. Which perceptual motor ability may be underdeveloped?

    a. Hearing

    b. Vision

    c. Touch sensitivity

    d. Audiation

4. Which of the following best describes the differences between motor learning and motor performance?

    a. Motor performance can be observed

    b. Motor learning can be observed

    c. Motor learning is the demonstration of motor skills

    d. Motor performance is permanent

5. Which of the following descriptions is most applicable to learning standards for PE students in grades 9-12?

    a. Students show the ability to explore fundamental locomotor and non-locomotor skills.

    b. Students are capable of demonstrating the mature forms in locomotor and non-locomotor skills.

    c. Students can apply the mature forms of motor skills in specialized sports, dance, and gymnastics.

    d. Students use locomotor, non-locomotor, manipulative skills in sports, dance, and gymnastics activities.

6. Among activities that demonstrate stability skills, which of these is developmentally appropriate for students in the second grade?

   a. Balancing and transferring weight on a beam
   b. Doing the stork stand, log roll, tumbling skills
   c. Walking on balance beam, 6" above the floor
   d. Balancing with partner, e.g., back-to-back sits

7. In a PE class, which of these would be an example of descriptive feedback?

   a. "Wow, way to go!"
   b. "Stand sideways!"
   c. "Use your instep!"
   d. "Follow through!"

8. Ms. Jones informed LaTonya that she did a good job keeping her eye on the ball but needed to strike the ball in front of her body. She pointed to the area that LaTonya should strike the ball and followed by stating, "strike sooner and keep up the great job tracking the ball." Which of the following feedback methods did Ms. Jones illustrate?

   a. the corrective method of feedback
   b. the constructive method of feedback
   c. the sandwich method of feedback
   d. the single channel method of feedback

9. Which of the following is an illustration of specific positive feedback?

   a. "Good job, Angela."
   b. "Angela, I like how you followed through."
   c. "Angela, keep up the good execution."
   d. "Angela, remember to follow through."

10. When does physical education instruction necessarily require giving feedback to students?

   a. When a skill requires specific correction
   b. When a skill gets environmental feedback
   c. When a student has experience with a skill
   d. When a teacher can comprehensively demonstrate a skill

11. Which of the following combined motor skills is on the upper end of the skill progression continuum?

   a. Skipping baseline to baseline
   b. Running 400 meters
   c. Dribbling a soccer ball
   d. Jumping over an obstacle

12. In three stages of motor learning, which of these is characteristic of the associative stage?

   a. Understanding an activity's goal and nature
   b. Making attempts that include major errors
   c. Making fewer and more consistent errors
   d. Effortless automaticity in performance

13. Among social, emotional, environmental, and health factors that affect motor development and performance, which of the following is the *best* example of the impact of social factors?

   a. A student's insecurities impede participation in physical activities.
   b. Many students would rather play video games than physical ones.
   c. Poor home living conditions limit student physical activity, fitness.
   d. A student's illness or disability makes physical activity challenging.

14. During what stage of motor development does talent begin to play a role?

   a. Stage 1
   b. Stage 2
   c. Stage 3
   d. Stage 4

15. High school students are computing their target heart rates for exercise. Which method takes into account individual differences?

   a. Standard method
   b. 65-85% method
   c. Pulse rate method
   d. Karvonen method

16. A century of research into motor development has yielded four major principles. Which choice most accurately reflects one of these principles?

   a. Children are like adults, only smaller.
   b. Children differ completely by gender.
   c. Children must earn things they want.
   d. Children have perfect bodies, or not.

17. Lisa is having difficulty balancing on one foot during her gymnastics routine. Which technique will help Lisa increase her stability?

   a. Follow the teacher or a classmate
   b. Keep her core engaged during the routine
   c. Practice balancing on one foot while stationary
   d. Practice balancing on one foot in short sequences

18. Which development in human manual skills emerges the earliest?

   a. Successfully reaching for objects
   b. Coordinated arm–hand movements
   c. Arm flapping and jerky arm extensions
   d. Changing hand shapes before touching objects

19. Which of the following best sums up the theory of deliberate practice?

   a. Practice makes perfect
   b. Natural athletes require little practice
   c. Long bouts of practice are most effective
   d. Reflection is a necessary aspect of practice

20. Which of these accurately reflects research findings on gender differences in early childhood motor development?

   a. Preschool girls are found to be equally muscular as, but more physically mature than, boys are in preschool.
   b. Preschool boys exhibit both more strength and coordination in large-muscle gross-motor skills than girls do.
   c. Preschool girls exhibit more fine-motor skills, but less gross-motor coordination, than boys do in preschool.
   d. Despite certain differences, preschool motor development between genders is more similar than different.

21. Which statement is true about children and environmental health risks?

   a. Children's body systems are more robust and resilient than adults' are.
   b. Children are liable to be more vulnerable to environmental health risks.
   c. Children take in fewer toxins from the air, water, and food than adults.
   d. Children's normal behaviors expose them to fewer toxins than adults'.

22. Which minimum daily amounts and types of physical activity are developmentally appropriate for developing cardiovascular endurance in young children?

   a. 30 minutes structured, 60 minutes unstructured daily for toddlers
   b. 30 minutes structured, 60 minutes unstructured for preschoolers
   c. 60 minutes structured, 60 minutes unstructured daily for toddlers
   d. 30 minutes structured, 30 minutes unstructured, both age groups

23. Where should a sprinter's center of gravity be to accelerate fastest out of the starting block?

   a. It should be as high as possible.
   b. It should be as low as possible.
   c. It should be right in the middle.
   d. It should be a full upright body.

24. A high school student learns the principle of available force, and by applying it, recognizes similarities among different sports. Which statement correctly reflects a related observation?

   a. In the broad jump, the takeoff can be too fast for the best force.
   b. In golf, the best results can be achieved by swinging the fastest.
   c. In this principle, variations in force and movement speed match.
   d. In the shot put, movement in the final thrust has no speed limit.

25. Which kinds of physical education activities are both appropriate for boys and girls to participate in together and are less dependent on team assignment by student skill levels?

   a. Activities that involve participant body contact
   b. Activities that require more upper-body strength
   c. Activities that require agility and lower-body strength
   d. Activities of all these types

26. How much physical activity is recommended for young children?

 a. A maximum of 30 minutes a day
 b. A minimum of two hours per day
 c. At most 15 minutes on most days
 d. At least 60 minutes on most days

27. Ms. Johnson is in a panic because Mr. Oliver took the heart rate monitors she needs for class. Which of the following heart rate monitoring strategies can the teacher use?

 a. taking the pulse rate at the radial artery
 b. using the talk test
 c. checking rate of perceived exertion
 d. asking students how they feel

28. Which of the following is an acute response to aerobic exercise?

 a. lower resting heart rate
 b. increase in ventilation
 c. constant cardiac output
 d. decrease in stroke volume

29. Jackson is doing extra cardiovascular exercises to compensate for the extra-large fries he ate during lunch. He wants to ensure his energy output and energy input are balanced. Which of the following principles or understandings is Jackson missing?

 a. one extra-large serving of fries is not that damaging
 b. he is accurate in his assessment given his youth
 c. exercise cannot compensate for a poor diet
 d. food quality is more critical than food quantity

30. Research shows that exercise lowers the risk of high blood pressure, stroke, and heart disease. What is true about other health benefits of exercise?

 a. Exercise lowers the risk of all kinds of cancers.
 b. Exercise cannot change the risk of dementia.
 c. Exercise lowers the risk for Type 1 diabetes.
 d. Exercise lowers the risk of breaking bones.

31. Which of the following fitness activities are students engaged in when participating in orienteering?

 a. Walking, hiking, and swimming
 b. Walking, cycling, and swimming
 c. Walking, jogging, and running
 d. Swimming, cycling, and running

32. Which of the following type of stress best describes anxiety a student experiences before participating in a fitness test?

 a. Eustress
 b. Distress
 c. Physical stress
 d. Fight or flight stress

33. In a risk management plan for a school PE program, which division or section would include emergency procedures and accident reports in cases of student injury?

    a. Conduct of activities and services
    b. Conditions from the environment
    c. Management of student behavior
    d. Practices of supervision in general

34. A spectator passes out during the football game and the CPR certified PE teacher is called to help. Which of the following steps should the PE teacher do first?

    a. call 911
    b. check the scene
    c. check for breathing
    d. start CPR

35. Jessie rolled his ankle after landing from a basketball rebound. Which of the following first aid treatment steps should be employed?

    a. elevating the injured area
    b. instructing Jessie to take off his shoe
    c. calling 911
    d. having Jessie walk to assess the injury

36. Which of the following best explains why people should not swim, hike, bike, or skate alone?

    a. To serve as a guide on directions
    b. To adhere to rules that govern each activity
    c. To utilize the buddy system
    d. To have someone present in case of an emergency

37. Which statement is correct regarding apparatus and procedures for testing sports equipment, specifically helmets?

    a. Auto crash simulation headforms are used to test linear impact from head collisions in football.
    b. Drop towers for testing helmet impact performance also apply with head collisions in football.
    c. The stretch in a helmet retention system is tested the same as the retention system's strength.
    d. The mouthguard on a helmet is designed to protect the teeth, not the brain from a concussion.

38. Which of the following should be a part of a school's emergency plan?

    a. First aid kit
    b. Exit routes
    c. Student medications
    d. Lesson plans

39. The cross-country coach had a spaghetti dinner for the team the night before a competition. Which of the following is the rationale for this activity?

    a. To recruit energy fast
    b. To run on an empty stomach
    c. To ensure an equitable, healthy meal
    d. To aid in better sleep

40. Which intensity of aerobic exercise have researchers found provides the greatest protection to the cardiovascular system against coronary heart disease specifically?

    a. Mild intensity
    b. Vigorous intensity
    c. Moderate intensity
    d. Any level of intensity

Subtest II: The Sociology and Psychology of Human Movement; Movement Concepts and Forms; Assessment and Evaluation of Principles

1. The teacher has chosen an activity where students write reflections on their pre-and post-fitness assessments. Which of the following describes the aim of this activity?

   a. To help students analyze performance
   b. To help students design a fitness program
   c. To help decrease the time of assessment
   d. To help students set fitness goals

2. Which of the following statements is most accurate about the role of self-assessment in developing physical fitness and lifelong participation in physical activity?

   a. Self-assessment should not be required since students lack the training.
   b. Self-assessment encourages reflection, which interferes with execution.
   c. Self-assessment enables students to determine their current skill levels.
   d. Self-assessment causes loss of control over the developmental process.

3. Which of the following best describes the purpose of the Presidential Youth Fitness and FitnessGram® programs?

   a. To assess health-related fitness
   b. To assess skill-related fitness
   c. To assess health- and skill-related fitness
   d. To assess dynamic fitness and sports skills

4. The teacher observes students daily and compares movement to the skill cues or model to provide student feedback. Which assessment strategy is the teacher using?

   a. Formative assessment
   b. Summative assessment
   c. Assessment for learning
   d. Assessment as learning

5. Which objective strategy helps students evaluate their cardiorespiratory fitness?

   a. The talk test
   b. Track resting heart rate
   c. Work at the target heart rate
   d. Reflection

6. Which of the following is an equitable fitness assessment?

   a. standardized fitness testing
   b. standards-based fitness goals
   c. fitness reflection journals
   d. peer-assessments

7. Spectators boo when a female golfer takes her stroke at a mixed-gender tournament. Which of the following behaviors are the spectators engaging in?

   a. taunting
   b. poor etiquette
   c. breaking the rules
   d. sexism

8. Bobby is unhappy that he lost his starting position and is lashing out at his replacement. Why should the coach work on teamwork strategies?

a. Teamwork aids in achieving team goals
b. Teamwork is required for success in life
c. Teamwork teaches responsibility
d. Teamwork teaches players about their role

9. Students in grades 9-12 should be able to do which of these with manipulative motor skills?

a. Refining and applying complex manipulative skills in lead-up games
b. Creating advanced movement skills and demonstrating using them
c. Demonstrating progress toward more manipulative skill complexity
d. Applying basic and advanced skills to sports, dance, and gymnastics

10. Of these, which one is classified as a locomotor skill?

a. Hopping
b. Bending
c. Twisting
d. Turning

11. Which of the following activities best illustrates manipulative skills?

a. Jumping and landing in the sand pit
b. Striking and kicking a ball
c. Running and jogging around the track
d. Bending and twisting high and low

12. Which of the following manipulative skills is NOT classified as propulsive?

a. Kicking
b. Striking
c. Catching
d. Throwing

13. A student is having difficulty staying afloat during the swimming unit. Which of the following identifies a potential problem and a solution to the student's issue?

a. The student has increased drag and needs to empty the air in their lungs
b. The student has high buoyancy and needs to empty the air in their lungs
c. The student lacks drag and needs to fill up their lungs with air
d. The student lacks buoyancy and needs to fill up their lungs with air

14. Which of the following indicates an effective muscular endurance training program?

a. Increasing the rep count over time
b. Increasing soreness over time
c. Maintaining the rep count over time
d. Increasing the weight over time

15. A healthy diet and regular engagement in physical activity help maintain a healthy body composition. Which type of physical activities have long-term calorie-burning effects after completion?

   a. Cardiovascular activities
   b. Stretching activities
   c. Pilates activities
   d. Resistance training activities

16. Which movement concept is the focus of locomotor and non-locomotor partner activities?

   a. Relationships
   b. High and low levels
   c. Lead-up activities for team sports
   d. Leading and following

17. Which of the following is the dominant movement concept when performing a leap?

   a. rhythm
   b. force
   c. time
   d. levels

18. Which category of skills best describes kicking and dribbling?

   a. Locomotor
   b. Non-locomotor
   c. Manipulative
   d. Closed skills

19. Among fundamental movement skills (FMS), which two are both part of the same main category?

   a. Locomotor and manipulative
   b. Manipulative and rotation
   c. Rotation and balance
   d. Balance and stability

20. Which of the following curriculum approaches focuses on the fundamental movement skills needed for advanced movement skills in sport and physical activities over the lifespan?

   a. Sport Education
   b. Teaching Games for Understanding
   c. Skill Themes
   d. Cooperative Learning

21. The teacher instructs students to dance freely in their coned-off areas. Which of the following spatial awareness concepts is the focus?

   a. personal space
   b. general space
   c. varying space
   d. non-locomotor space

22. You want to develop students' object control and locomotor skills. Which of the following is the BEST way to do this?
   a. Require the students to describe shot put technique
   b. Ask the students to throw a Frisbee
   c. Lead the students in different kinds of dance
   d. Have the students play a game of catch

23. Which of the following should the teacher first consider during long-term planning of outdoor lessons?
   a. Temperature
   b. Playing surface
   c. Supervision
   d. Boundaries

24. Of the following statements, which is true about aerobics?
   a. Aerobics originally focused on the flexibility of the body.
   b. Aerobics originally focused on the strength of the muscles.
   c. Aerobics originally focused on cardiorespiratory endurance.
   d. Aerobics originally focused on one thing as it still does today.

25. Which of the following is a defensive running pattern common in dual and team sports?
   a. high level
   b. zigzags
   c. transitions
   d. curves

26. Which of the following best describes the grapevine step?
   a. Step touch right, step touch left. step touch right, tap
   b. Step forward, step backward, step right, tap
   c. Step, hop, step, tap
   d. Step, cross, step, tap

27. Jumping fast and landing softly best describe which movement concepts?
   a. Strong and weak
   b. Strong and forceful
   c. Tempo and force
   d. Time and speed

28. Kimberly is not demonstrating opposition during the overhand throw. Which of the following techniques will promote the desired outcome?
   a. Telling her she needs to step with the opposite foot
   b. Telling her to practice daily
   c. Telling her to work with a partner
   d. The teacher should recognize that all students will not master every skill and move on

29. A bowler is capable of hitting the middle pin relatively consistently. What is one way they can improve their success at making strikes?

    a. Using a heavier ball
    b. Moving further to the left
    c. Putting more spin on the ball
    d. Throwing the ball from farther away

30. Lena is a back row player in volleyball. Her bump/forearm pass keeps going into the net. Which of the following cues will help Lena correct her error?

    a. "Swing your arms."
    b. "Bend at the knees."
    c. "Face the net."
    d. "Let the libero take the pass."

31. Mr. Jackson is excited to try out new teambuilding activities that he learned during the physical education professional development. Which of the following strategies foster teamwork?

    a. Trust falls
    b. Taking turns
    c. Allowing students to pick teams
    d. Rotating team captains

32. Which of the following best describes the health effect of consuming excessive amounts of alcohol and smoking tobacco?

    a. Increased risk of eating disorders
    b. Increased risk of a sedentary lifestyle
    c. Increased risk of heart disease
    d. Increased risk of obesity

33. Four developmental levels of student personal and social responsibility in PE have been identified (Hellison, 1995). To facilitate student growth by building on student strengths, at which level would it be appropriate for a PE teacher to use a peer teaching strategy to increase student interaction?

    a. Level 1, Self-control
    b. Level 0, Irresponsibility
    c. Level 2, Involvement
    d. Level 4, Caring

34. Researchers studying how PE teachers can influence student self-determination found all of these EXCEPT which choice?

    a. Teachers' supporting student autonomy was motivating.
    b. Teachers' furnishing students structure motivated them.
    c. Teachers' self-determination affected their involvement.
    d. Teachers' self-determination predicted that of students.

35. Which of the following BEST describes how participation in physical education can improve a student's self-esteem?
   a. It can teach students new or improved skills.
   b. It can foster a sense of wonder at human athleticism.
   c. It can teach students to take turns when playing sports/games.
   d. It can cause the release of endorphins, natural "feel good" chemicals.

36. The teacher has created progressive activities where students easily find success in skill acquisition before moving on to more complex skills. Which of the following concepts is developed through this practice?
   a. emotional development
   b. self-regulation
   c. motivation competence
   d. autonomous development

37. Student-centered instructional approaches have been shown to be more effective than teacher-driven approaches. Which of the following student-centered approaches has been shown to increase motivation?
   a. Choice
   b. Direct instruction
   c. Competition
   d. Traditional

38. Which of the following activities fosters motivation to engage in lifelong physical activity?
   a. Grades
   b. Fitness testing
   c. Self-assessment
   d. Ability tracking

39. Which of these is a typical effect of substance abuse on student behavior?
   a. A shy student becomes more sociable.
   b. An outgoing student becomes withdrawn.
   c. An inhibited student becomes more impulsive.
   d. These are all typical effects of substance abuse.

40. Various studies of youth development results of sports-based life skills programs have found improvement in which outcomes for BOTH 10- to 12-year-old AND adolescent participants?
   a. Social responsibility
   b. Positive thinking
   c. Problem solving
   d. Goal setting

Subtest III: Professional Foundations; Integration of Concepts

1. Out of 30 students, 10 are advanced, 10 are intermediate, and 10 are beginners. Which of the following strategies best accommodates mixed-ability students for skill development and refinement?

    a. Skill choice
    b. Varied skill circuits
    c. Combined skill grouping
    d. Partner advanced and beginner students

2. A student recovering from a knee injury has medical clearance to engage in physical education. Which of the following modifications are recommended for cardiovascular activities?

    a. Excuse the student from exercises that involve jumps
    b. Allow the student to choose from a list of exercises
    c. Refrain from activities until the knee has completely healed
    d. Allow the student to assess peers in cardiovascular activities

3. Kevin meets the objectives of hand dribbling while running and changing directions. Which of the following task modifications can the teacher employ that will challenge Kevin?

    a. dribbling with a defender
    b. dribbling around cones
    c. dribbling with two basketballs
    d. moving to the next objective of shooting

4. Which of the following explains the importance of discipline when engaging in recreational activities?

    a. The rules of engagement are unclear.
    b. There is no one to monitor activity.
    c. The outcome goals are unclear.
    d. Goals vary for each individual.

5. Which of the following health benefits result from regular engagement in muscular fitness activities?

    a. Increases aerobic capacity
    b. Bone density loss prevention
    c. Reduces the risk of cardiovascular disease
    d. Reduces the risk of some cancers

6. Which of the following best explains the rationale behind physical education promoting physical activity over the lifespan?

    a. Lowers the risk of heart disease
    b. Increases blood pressure
    c. Responsible for muscle atrophy
    d. Decreases endorphins

7. Among examples of how physical education (PE) teachers can collaborate with other educators, which one applies most to taking advantage of administrator support to improve student motivation and learning?

    a. Reading *A River Runs Through It* to study fly-fishing and character development and relationships

    b. Watching *Footloose* to study dance movements and themes of freedom, rebellion, and repression

    c. Designing a joint PE and Family and Consumer Sciences unit that combines nutrition and exercise

    d. Developing a morning walk/run project together with the principal to help students focus better

8. A student consistently engages in low-intensity cardiovascular activities during class and has low performance on the cardiovascular assessments. Which of the following recommendations may help this student increase intensity and improve?

    a. Interval training with heart rate tracking

    b. Using a pedometer with step count goal

    c. Listing the benefits of cardiovascular health

    d. Engaging in activity for longer periods of time

9. Which of the following best illustrates the impact hearing has on learning a dance sequence?

    a. The sound of music informs the learner of the tempo of the dance sequence

    b. The sound of music has little impact on the ability to learn a dance sequence

    c. The sound of music informs when the learner performs the steps in a dance sequence

    d. The sound of music may confuse the learner's ability to learn a dance sequence

10. Which of the following correctly reflects research findings about the relationship of exercise to stress?

    a. Aerobic exercise can elevate but not stabilize mood.

    b. Aerobic exercise can enhance sleep and self-esteem.

    c. Aerobic exercise can reduce anxiety if performed more than 10 minutes.

    d. Aerobic exercise can aid cognition yet cause fatigue.

11. Which of the following is a physiological benefit of exercise that helps manage stress responses?

    a. it improves mood

    b. it enhances positive thoughts

    c. it lowers the release of cortisol

    d. it increases confidence

12. Which of the following is a strategy used for refinement and integration of manipulative skills?

    a. mirroring

    b. choice

    c. leading and following

    d. small-sided games

13. Research finds that motor skills training, endurance training, and strength training all share which neuroplasticity effects in common?

   a. New blood vessel formation
   b. Motor map reorganization
   c. Spinal reflex modification
   d. New synapse generation

14. Related to summation of forces, which is accurate about how body parts move?

   a. The largest body parts are the slowest and move last.
   b. The smallest body parts are the fastest and move first.
   c. The largest body parts are the slowest and move first.
   d. Regardless of speed, all parts move at the same times.

15. What advantages does Fitbit technology include for physical education teachers and students?

   a. Weight control but not sleep quality
   b. Self-monitoring but not competition
   c. Fashion appeal as well as motivation
   d. Stand-alone fitness progress tracking

16. The English literature department has decided that Harry Potter is the book that all 6th graders will read this year. The department chair asks the PE teachers to reinforce concepts from the book in class. Which of the following approaches best describes this request?

   a. Tactical approach
   b. Integrated approach
   c. Cooperative games approach
   d. Skill themes approach

17. In general, when demonstrating PE skills or skill combinations, which principle applies most?

   a. Demonstrate the skill as whole-part-whole.
   b. Demonstrate only a skill's component parts.
   c. Demonstrate the entire skill only as a whole.
   d. Demonstrate by giving more, not fewer, cues.

18. Which of the following steps used in jazz dance is similar to the gallop?

   a. chasse
   b. axel
   c. ball change
   d. the drop

19. For fifth-grade students, which of the following shows the ability to integrate locomotor, non-locomotor, and stability movements within more complex movement skills?

   a. Showing mature motor patterns on obstacle courses
   b. Playing simple games that require manipulative skills
   c. Describing the important parts of throwing overhand
   d. Understanding that practicing improves performance

20. The President's Council on Physical Fitness and Sports identifies personal development benefits of PE as well as physiological health benefits. The former include which of the following as social and psychological life skills rather than improved developmental outcomes?

   a. Showing self-confidence
   b. Showing peer resistance
   c. Showing self-regulation
   d. Showing perseverance

21. Callie slips on the spilled water on the gym floor and breaks her arm during physical education class. Which of the following violations has occurred?

   a. Accountability
   b. Misfeasance
   c. Negligence
   d. Malfeasance

22. According to national physical education (PE) standards, to show respect, which of the following should PE teachers do to address a student's behavior problem?

   a. The teacher describes the student's behavior, why it was disruptive, and solutions for the problem.
   b. The teacher has a classmate describe the behavior, why it was disruptive, and solutions for the problem.
   c. The teacher has the student describe the behavior, why it was disruptive, and solutions for the problem.
   d. The teacher avoids discussing it but provides concrete consequences and solutions for the problem.

23. Which level is primarily responsible for the development of physical education standards in the United States of America?

   a. National organizations
   b. State education agencies
   c. Physical education teachers
   d. School districts

24. Physical education is under attack by a powerful parent group who believe physical education is only fun and games. Which of the following laws can be used to explain to parents the impact of physical education?

   a. Title IX
   b. IDEA
   c. SHAPE America toolkit
   d. ESSA

25. A closeted homosexual student comes out in confidence to the physical education teacher. What should the teacher do with this information?

   a. Contact the student's parents
   b. Contact the student's school counselor
   c. Keep quiet to maintain student trust
   d. Encourage the student to come out to peers

26. The Society of Health and Physical Educators (SHAPE America) offers tools for advocates of PE. Which of the following among these tools could an advocate best use to show stakeholders and decision makers why and how school health and physical education is important and beneficial for all students?

   a. *The Essential Components of Physical Education,* guidance document
   b. *PE + Health = Student Success   (Speak Out! for Health & PE)*, fact sheet
   c. *Physical Education is an Academic Subject*, SHAPE position statement
   d. *Advocacy in Action* columns from SHAPE America's *Strategies* journal

27. The teacher thinks a student is fabricating the need to get his inhaler during the mile run and does not allow him to get it. The student ignores the denial, retrieves the inhaler, and reports the teacher. Which of the following legal or ethical issues might the teacher encounter?

   a. assumption of risk
   b. breach of duty
   c. proximate cause
   d. damages

28. A male student wants to join the dance team. His parents are extremely dissatisfied and think boys should play football. What strategy can the teacher use to support the student without offending the parents?

   a. Respectfully tell the parents they are misinformed
   b. Suggest that the student participate in both
   c. Discuss the risks of playing football
   d. Discuss the physical benefits of dance

29. Regarding inherent risks of participating in some physical activities in a school PE program, school risk management plans typically include an Agreement to Participate form at the beginning of the school year, term, or semester. Which parties are typically required to sign this form?

   a. Students and their parents or guardians
   b. Only students' parents or guardians are
   c. Only the students are required to sign it
   d. Students, their parents, and PE teachers

30. A physical education program has a 4:1 student-equipment ratio, a large teaching area, a class size of 38-42 students, and students are engaged at least 50% of the time. Which of the following elements of an effective physical education program is present and appropriately accounted for in the example?

   a. equipment ratio and teaching area
   b. class size and student engagement
   c. student engagement and equipment ratio
   d. student engagement and teaching area

31. Which of the following is an example of a SHAPE America grade level outcome?

   a. The student will recognize value in physical activity
   b. The student will demonstrate motor skills
   c. The student will apply movement concepts
   d. The student will skip using a mature pattern

32. Which of the following agencies set the goals and curricula for state-level K-12 physical education?

    a. SHAPE
    b. CAEP
    c. HPE
    d. ESSA

33. Some students with obese body mass indices are reluctant to participate during the fitness activities but are actively engaged in team sports as indicated on their heart rate monitors during game play. Which of the following can the teacher do to increase fitness participation among these students?

    a. focus on health
    b. focus on standards
    c. focus on competitive fitness activities
    d. focus on body composition

34. Concerning the impacts of various resources on student physical education (PE) outcomes, what has research found?

    a. Class size and student–teacher ratio correlate inversely with activity levels, time, safety, and learning.
    b. Students receive a higher quantity and quality of PE from teachers who also teach different subjects.
    c. Student physical activity is the same whether PE curriculum is based on educational standards or not.
    d. PE facilities and equipment are valuable resources but do not change the amount of student activity.

35. After tracking his teaching behaviors, Mr. Green realized that taking attendance for 40 students takes up a lot of time, which reduces student engagement. How might Mr. Green alter his attendance taking method to increase the opportunities for students to respond?

    a. set a time-limit to take attendance
    b. practice taking attendance faster
    c. take attendance during the warm-up
    d. take attendance in squad lines

36. A physical education teacher designs a student volleyball activity to meet National Association for Sport and Physical Education (NASPE) standards for setting, spiking, forearm passing, defensive strategies, officiating; aerobic capacity; and cooperating and accepting challenges. Which of the following represents the correct sequence of steps in this activity?

    a. Rotational positions; serve; base positions; defend against attack
    b. Base positions; rotational positions; defend against attack; serve
    c. Serve; base positions; defend against attack; rotational positions
    d. Defend against attack; serve; rotational positions; base positions

37. Professional development at its best accomplishes which of these?

    a. Improves primarily the teacher's own knowledge and skills
    b. Improves both a teacher's and his or her colleagues' expertise
    c. Improves primarily the expertise of the teacher's colleagues
    d. Improves teaching practices primarily at the classroom level

38. Among elements of the FITT principle, which one is determined by two of the others?

a. How long each workout session should last
b. How to ensure overload without overwork
c. How often to work out for stress plus rest
d. How training is cardio, resistance, or both

39. A teacher noticed that a student comes to school with random bruises on their body. The teacher inquires, and the student indicates that their stepfather uses his fists as a discipline method. Which of the following steps should the teacher take?

a. Contact the child's mother to verify the child's claims
b. Keep quiet to maintain trust
c. Begin the reporting process
d. Take photos of the injuries for evidence

40. Compared to the amount of time in moderate to vigorous physical activity (MVPA) the Institute of Medicine recommends for children to spend daily, how much do research studies find they actually spend in school physical education classes?

a. About one-sixth of what is recommended
b. About one-third of what is recommended
c. About one-half of what is recommended
d. About the same as is recommended

Answer Key and Explanations

Subtest I: Growth, Motor Development, and Motor Learning; The Science of Human Movement

1. A: A child with Attention Deficit Hyperactivity Disorder (ADHD) who becomes exhausted from engaging in excessive physical activity is an example of an emotional (and behavioral) condition that can affect levels of physical activity and fitness. A child with depression who avoids physical activity is also an example of this. The need to monitor a child with asthma for breathing problems during exercise (B) is an example of how a physical factor can affect physical activity and fitness levels, as are the need to monitor the exercise of a child with diabetes and coordinate it with the child's diet (C), and a physically disabled child's need for adaptive equipment (and/or alternative instructional methods) to participate in physical activities (D).

2. D: In Stage 1 of motor learning, babies and toddlers develop beyond simple reflexive movements (e.g., rooting, sucking, startling, Babinski, Moro, palmar, plantar) to fundamental purposeful movements like sitting, crawling, standing, and walking. In Stage 2, young children develop more complex motor patterns (b), like running, climbing, jumping, balancing, catching, and throwing. In Stage 3, older children develop greater automaticity and fluidity in performing the Stage 2 motor patterns (c) while learning more specific movement skills. In Stage 4, adolescents master specialized movements while ability, motivation, and practice influence continuing general and specific motor skills development (d).

3. B: Vision is the perceptual motor ability that aids in movement detection and movement response. If Kenya is closing her eyes, that may be causing increased balance and coordination difficulty, as those sensory responses are not activated. Hearing perception is important for motor skill development but is more closely related to the body preparing to take action, for example, when hearing "go" or "start," or the sound of a thrown or caught ball.

4. A: Motor performance can be observed, but motor learning cannot. Observing motor performance over time can aid in the determination of motor learning. Motor learning is permanent, e.g., riding a bicycle; however, motor performance changes based on the environment such as lack of rest or facing a tough defender.

5. D: Exploring the basics of these skills (a) most applies to students in grades K-2. Demonstrating mature forms of these skills (b) most applies to students in grades 3-5. Applying those mature forms in more specialized PE areas (c) most applies to students in grades 6-8. Using these motor skills for activities in these areas (d) most applies to students in grades 9-12.

6. C: Balancing and transferring weight on a beam (a) or performing a stork stand, log roll, or other simple tumbling skill (b) are developmentally appropriate for students in kindergarten. Simple partnered balancing, as in back-to-back sits (d), is developmentally appropriate for students in the first grade. Walking end to end on a balance beam 6" above the floor (c) without touching the floor or anything else is developmentally appropriate for students in the second grade.

7. A: In PE classes, feedback is typically **descriptive**, i.e., general and vague, like (a), or **prescriptive**, i.e., specific and instructive. General praise can be reinforcing socially, but does not tell the student what to do or how to do it. Prescriptive feedback helps students learn motor skills correctly, e.g., giving direction for proper baseball batting or tennis rallying stance (b), kicking technique (c), or technical tips for effective batting, hitting, throwing, kicking, etc. (d).

8. C: The sandwich method of feedback puts constructive or corrective feedback between two positive comments or feedback. The sandwich method increases motivation, as constructive or corrective criticism can demotivate students as they tend to view it as negative. The positive comments should be specific and highlight what the student is doing well. The corrective feedback should also be specific and include the desired outcome. Pointing out wrong or incorrect movements can demotivate students. Single-channel feedback is a motor behavior theory which posits that people can only focus on one thing at a time, so it is better not to focus on too many feedback cues at once.

9. B: "Angela, I like how you followed through" is an example of specific positive feedback. The student's name was used, followed by a positive comment on a specific part of the skill. Stating "good job" is vague and does not inform the student what was good about their performance. "Keep up the good execution" is also vague because there are several steps in a skill that need to executed. Reminding a student of a skill cue is corrective feedback that suggests the student is not doing this action.

10. A: While feedback is important in physical education (PE) instruction, knowing when and when not to provide feedback is equally important to effective teaching. PE teachers need to give feedback to give students specific corrections to incorrectly performed techniques, for example. However, when a task furnishes inherent environmental feedback (B),—for example, a student throws a basketball, and it goes through the hoop—additional feedback may be unnecessary. When a student already has enough experience with a skill (C), sometimes PE teachers need not give them feedback. Also, when a teacher's demonstration enables students to see easily how to perform a skill correctly (D), they may need little or no additional feedback.

11. C: Dribbling a soccer ball is on the upper end of the skill progression continuum, as it combines a locomotor movement with an object (a manipulative skill), and is one of the most difficult fundamental movement skills. Skipping, running, and jumping are basic locomotor or fundamental movements.

12. C: In the first, cognitive stage of motor learning, learners understand the activity's goal and nature (A) and make initial attempts to perform it that include major errors (B). In the second, associative stage, learners engage in practice to master the timing of the skill, and they make fewer errors that are more consistent in nature (C). In the third, autonomous stage, learners perform the activity effortlessly and automatically (D), enabling them to redirect their attention to other aspects of the skill.

13. B: When participating in PE or other physical activity is impeded by student insecurities (a), this is an example of the impact of psychological factors on motor development and performance. The widespread phenomenon of playing video games to the exclusion of physical ones (b) is the best example of the impact of social factors. Poor home living conditions (c) are an example of the impact of environmental factors. Illnesses and disabilities (d) are examples of health factors.

14. D: It is during Stage 4 that talent, among other factors, plays a role in how a person continues to develop motor skills. Other relevant factors include how highly a person is motivated and how often a person practices the motor skills in question. Stage 4 is the last stage of motor development, during which one hones existing skills, as well as learns more complicated skills (for example, refining a golf swing to hit the ball in just the right way). In prior stages of motor development, talent does not play a particular role in how a person develops motor skills.

15. D: The Karvonen method for computing target heart rate (THR) zones is considered the best because it takes into account the age and resting heart rate of an individual, which is an indicator of cardiovascular fitness and more accurately estimates a person's THR. The standard method only takes age into account. Using the standard method ([220–age] × 65% and [220–age] × 85%), for example, an 18-year-old with a 68-bpm resting heart rate would have a THR of 131-172 bpm. Using the Karvonen method ([[(220–age–RHR) × 65%+RHR] and [(220–age–RHR) × 85%+RHR]]), the same individual would have a THR of 155-182 bpm, which illustrates a higher range given the resting heart rate. Pulse rate methods only provide the number of heart beats, which are used to determine what the pulse is, not what pulse should be targeted. The 65-85% option is not a method but rather the range for someone's THR, regardless of the method employed. Sedentary individuals may work at 50-60% and gradually build up, while elite exercisers may work at the 90% threshold.

16. C: Four major principles of motor development are: children are NOT miniature adults (a); among children, boys and girls are more similar than different (b); children get good things by earning them (c); and nobody, and no body, is perfect (d). (a), (b), and (d) each contradict one of these principles; (c) reflects one of them more accurately than the others.

17. D: Lisa should practice balancing on one foot in short sequences or sections, and gradually increase to the complete routine. This technique is known as chunking, which will help Lisa prepare for the dynamic movements involved in the full routine (running, jumping, landing). Practicing balancing in isolation does not provide Lisa the opportunity to develop or engage in muscle recruitment and strength building needed to maintain balance.

18. B: Human babies actually display coordinated arm–hand movements in the womb before birth, such as moving their thumbs to their mouths. The amniotic fluid provides buoyancy to make this easier. After birth, gravity makes arm and hand movements harder for newborns, who initially exhibit arm flapping and jerky arm extensions (C) before progressing to successfully reaching for objects (A) around four to five months old. At this age, they only adjust their hand shapes to object shapes after touching them. They develop the ability to use visual information to change their hand shapes before touching objects (D) around the age of eight months.

19. D: The primary principle of the theory of deliberate practice is that practicing a skill needs to be a focused and reflective process. If the student is not deliberate, or focused on making progress, the student's volume of practice will not be enough to improve their skill level. A secondary principal of deliberate practice is that there needs to be much practice to see effective gains. Regardless of students' ability levels, including the ability level of those who are natural athletes, lots of practice is required to achieve mastery. Short bouts of regular practice have shown to be the most effective method of skill mastery. While some believe that practice makes perfect, performing a skill incorrectly repeatedly will negate mastery of the desired skill. "Perfect practice makes perfect" would be more appropriate.

20. D: Researchers have observed consistent gender differences in preschool physical and motor development; however, they also observe that in spite of these differences, overall the physical and motor development of preschoolers is more similar than different between genders. In general, the differences are not significant enough to place any emphasis on motor development differences between preschool boys and girls. Some known differences, however, include that preschool boys are more muscular than preschool girls, but preschool girls are more physically mature than preschool boys (A). While preschool boys exhibit more strength in large-muscle, gross-motor skills, preschool girls exhibit more coordination in large-muscle, gross-motor skills (B and C). Additionally, preschool girls are superior to preschool boys in fine-motor skills as well as gross-motor coordination (C).

21. B: Children are liable to be more vulnerable to environmental health risks than adults for several reasons. For one, children's body systems are immature and are still developing, making them easier to damage than those of adults, not vice versa (A). For another, children have smaller body sizes than adults do, so they take in more not fewer (C) toxins through the air they breathe, the water they drink, and the foods they eat. Additionally, the normal behaviors of children expose them to more, not fewer (D) toxins than normal adult behaviors do. Children are more likely to handle and mouth unsanitary and toxic substances and objects; to engage in physical contact with others having contagious illnesses; to go without washing their hands before and after using the bathroom, eating, etc.; to expose themselves unwittingly to various environmental toxins; and to lack experience and judgment about exposure.

22. A: Experts recommend toddlers have at least 30 minutes of structured physical activity (PA) and at least 60 minutes of unstructured PA daily. For preschoolers, the recommendation is 60 minutes of structured PA and at least 60 minutes of unstructured PA daily, not 30/60 (b); hence 60/60 is NOT advised for toddlers (c). The recommendations are NOT the same for both age groups (d), and 30 minutes of unstructured PA is insufficient for either.

23. A: To attain the fastest acceleration, a sprinter should keep the center of gravity as high as possible while crouching in the starting block. As the sprinter accelerates, the upper body rises with forward body propulsion. Having the center of gravity lowest (b), between high and low (c), or starting in the full upright body position (d) will allow less speed in accelerating.

24. A: According to the principle of available force, movement speed and available force have an inverse relationship; i.e., as one increases, the other decreases; thus (c) is incorrect. This principle explains, in part, similarities among sports that the student in the question recognizes: taking off too fast in the broad jump can reduce force, hence distance (a); NOT swinging too fast gets better results in golf (b); and movement speed has a limit in the shot put (d).

25. C: Activities that require agility and lower-body strength, which do not involve body contact (A), are most appropriate for coed participation and are less dependent on team assignment by student skill levels. For activities that require more upper-body strength (B), it is more important for physical education teachers to assign teams according to individual student skill levels to prevent injuries. Therefore, (D) is incorrect.

26. D: Experts recommend that young children have at least 60 minutes of physical activity on most days. This is important for strengthening bones, muscles including the heart, and lungs; developing gross motor skills; ensuring better sleep; developing social skills; reinforcing family bonds through family playtimes; having fun and improving children's moods; and boosting children's self-images and self-esteem through pride at physical attainments. Minimums of 30 (A) or 15 (C) minutes are not enough physical activity for young children; two hours (B) can be excessive at this age.

27. A: Ms. Johnson can have students take their pulse at the radial or carotid arteries to measure heart rate. The talk test helps determine if the activities are too easy or intense, but it does not measure heart rate. The rate of perceived exertion is another tool used to determine or evaluate the intensity of exercises but is not a heart rate measurement. Asking students how they feel is a great tool to check in to assess students' responses to activities but is not a tool to measure heart rate.

28. B: An increase in ventilation or breathing is an acute or immediate response to aerobic exercise. A lower resting heart rate is a long-term physiological response to aerobic exercise. Cardiac output remains constant during long sessions of aerobic exercise. Cardiac output and stroke volume (the amount of blood ejected from the left and right ventricle due to the contraction of the heart) increases are also acute responses to aerobic exercise.

29. C: Jackson is missing that exercise cannot compensate for a poor diet as excessive fat intake can clog the arteries even with energy balanced. Many comorbidity diseases start to develop during the teen years and manifest or appear in adulthood. Youth and poor dietary habits having little effect on health are a myth. Food quality and food quantity are both important, but a high quantity of high-quality foods such as cruciferous vegetables are better than the same quantity of low-quality foods like French fries. Moderation is recommended for low-quality food intake; however, French fries are noted as one of the worst foods to eat, even in moderation, as they have been linked to obesity, diabetes, and cardiovascular disease at a three times higher rate than baked potatoes. A skinless potato also has little nutritional value and a high glycemic index, which contributes to disease risk.

30. D: Research proves weight-bearing exercise strengthens bones, lowering risk for osteoporosis and associated bone fractures. Exercise lowers risk for colon cancer, breast cancer, and some others, but is not proven to lower risk for every kind of cancer (a). It lowers risk for Alzheimer's-type dementia including memory loss (b), as well as depression. It lowers risk for Type 2 diabetes, not Type 1 (Type 1 has a stronger genetic component, so even physically active children can develop it; however, carefully monitored and controlled exercise helps them manage this condition).

31. C: Students engage in walking, jogging, and running when engaged in orienteering. In a triathlon, fitness activities include swimming, cycling, and running or jogging. Hiking, swimming, and cycling benefit muscular and cardiovascular fitness but are not skills used in orienteering.

32. B: Distress is a form of stress that leads to anxiety or extreme nervousness. Eustress is positive stress and is often felt prior to a physical performance (game, dance, or music recital); however, these events can also bring on distress—usually among individuals with low competence or confidence. Physical stress can be positive (physical activity needed for positive physiological adaptations) and negative (headache, pain). Fight or flight is a stress response. Some avoid dealing with stressful situations (flight) while others persevere (fight). Allowing students several opportunities to practice fitness tests helps reduce stress and anxiety.

33. D: In a typical school PE risk management plan, General Supervisory Practices includes subcategories of Risk Management Planning Dimensions; Management of Student Behavior (c) / Rules and Regulations; Security; and Care of Injured and Emergency Procedures. Conduct of Activities and Services (a) includes Adequacy of Instruction and Progress; Use of Warnings and Participation Forms; Maturity and Condition of Participants; and Transportation of Students. Environmental Conditions (b) includes Equipment; Facility Layout; Area and Facility Maintenance; and Health Hazards.

34. B: The PE teacher should first check the scene for safety. Next, she would check the spectator for signs of consciousness, e.g., talking, breathing, and pulse. If there is no breathing, the PE teacher would identify and instruct someone to call 911 and include the assessment. If there is an AED available, that request would also be made followed by CPR until the AED arrives, medical personnel arrive, and/or the PE teacher is too tired to continue performing CPR correctly.

35. A: Jessie should elevate the injured area to reduce swelling and inflammation. It would be better for Jessie to keep his shoe on for support, compression, and inflammation reduction. Removing his shoe may increase the risk of swelling and further injury. A call to 911 would occur for a severe or life-threatening injury. Jessie should sit down or rest the injured area, as walking can cause further damage.

36. D: Swimming, hiking, biking, or skating with a companion allows someone to be present in case of an emergency. Avid swimmers can get a cramp or other injury in the water or go into cardiac arrest, which increases drowning risks. It is wise to swim at pools and beaches that have lifeguards. Runners, hikers, and skaters can sprain or break an ankle, fall, or have an accident with a motor vehicle. While wearing a helmet is recommended when biking and skating, it is not a law in many states, or there is little to no penalty for not wearing one.

37. A: Companies like Biokinetics (www.biokinetics.com) use different machinery, software, and procedures to test sports equipment like helmets against official standards. While drop tests from towers traditionally test helmet impact performance, this method cannot accurately test football head-to-head collision impacts (b) because players collide at much higher speeds; linear impact tests, with rams hitting auto crash-simulation headforms, are used (a). Different tests and apparatus test helmet retention system stretch rather than strength and stability (c). Helmet mouthguards not only protect teeth, but also brains from concussions (d); headforms with articulating mandibles test this.

38. B: Exit routes should be included and posted as part of the teacher's emergency plan. The emergency plan may include the first aid kit's location and how to treat injuries, but the first aid kit alone (A) is not a part of an emergency plan. Student medications (C) such as an inhaler or epi-pen, should either be with the student, school nurse, teacher, or central location for easy retrieval. The teacher should be aware of students with medical conditions, ensure that students have appropriate medications before activity engagement, and be certified in first aid and CPR. Medical conditions and how to treat them are generally in the teacher's notes or lesson plan (D), but generally not included in the emergency plan—as emergency plans are designed to address general, school-wide emergencies, such as a fire or an intruder, and the steps to take, rather than addressing specific needs of individual students.

39. A: Eating a high carbohydrate meal, also known as carb loading, before an endurance activity is done for fast and easy recruitment of glucose and glycogen energy rather than waiting 20-minutes for the fat energy stores to become available, which could slow down a runner's pace. If running on an empty stomach, the body will need to recruit stored glucose (glycogen). While glycogen is a faster energy source than fats, glucose obtained from a light snack or breakfast is more ideal as it is already in the bloodstream and does not need to metabolize or be broken down like glycogen and stored fat. The meal is equitable but that is not the most important reason for eating a high carbohydrate meal before an endurance activity. Depending on the time the meal is eaten, it may help or hurt sleep, but it is not the purpose of carb loading.

40. B: While even mild (a) exercise is better than none, and moderate (c) exercise prevents a great variety of illnesses, researchers have found aerobic exercise at a vigorous intensity level the most beneficial specifically to protect the cardiovascular system against coronary heart disease. Therefore, (d) is incorrect.

Subtest II: The Sociology and Psychology of Human Movement; Movement Concepts and Forms; Assessment and Evaluation of Principles

1. A: The purpose of this reflection in pre- and post-fitness assessments is to help students analyze performance and compare the results. The analysis needs to transpire first before students can set fitness goals. Students can start to design a fitness program after the development of fitness goals. Reflections increase the assessment time since the teacher would have to read through the reflection responses to determine if students are adequate in their analysis.

2. C: According to PE experts, self-assessment has great power as a tool in student motor skills development, because requiring students to assess their own abilities and skills encourages them to reflect, which does NOT interfere with executing the skills (b), but does enable them to determine their current skill levels (c), as well as to take, not lose, control of the developmental process (d). Students need not be PE teachers or have specialized training to conduct self-assessment (a).

3. A: The Presidential Youth Fitness and FitnessGram® programs are designed to assess health-related fitness, including muscular endurance, muscular strength, cardiovascular endurance, flexibility, and body composition, as these components impact life quality. Skill-related fitness (B) is sport-related or performance skills and includes power, agility, coordination, speed, reaction time, and balance. Fitness assessments that measure both skills- and health-related fitness (C) are assessments used for military entry and training, including the candidate fitness test. Dynamic and non-dynamic or static activities (D) are conducted in the Presidential Youth and FitnessGram® assessments but do not include sports skills.

4. A: The teacher is demonstrating a type of formative assessment, which is used to identify student strengths and weaknesses, and provide feedback on how to improve or refine. Formative assessment is also called assessment *of* learning, whereas assessment *for* learning is summative assessment, which identifies what students have learned and comes at the end of the unit or lesson. Assessment *as* learning are self-assessments that students engage in to monitor their own progress and make changes accordingly, which aid in deepening understanding of the tasks.

5. B: Students can evaluate their cardiorespiratory fitness by tracking their resting heart rate over time. As cardiorespiratory fitness increases, resting and exercise heart rates decrease. To improve cardiovascular fitness, students should work at their target heart rate zone. The talk test is a subjective measure that is used during cardiovascular activity to gauge intensity. Reflections can be used to aid in the evaluation but may include subjective and objective data. A subjective data example may include students reporting how they felt during the activity by stating something like, "I can tell that my cardiorespiratory fitness is improving because I was not out of breath." An objective data example may be students reporting their heart rate data in their journals. Regardless of the method, criteria need to be set for evaluating cardiorespiratory fitness.

6. C: Allowing students to reflect on their individual fitness is an equitable approach as students can focus on their personal goals and needs. Students can develop personal goals, create a plan, determine how to assess/track/monitor, and adjust accordingly. Standardized fitness testing and standards-based fitness goals are not equitable as all students are expected to meet a standard not tailored to the individual.

7. B: Spectators are engaging in poor etiquette as it is an expectation that fans and spectators are quiet during stokes. Booing at any moment during a golf tournament is also considered poor etiquette. Taunting is intentional behavior designed to insult or provoke someone. The spectators are not breaking any rules, but the practice of booing is strongly discouraged and considered poor taste. While the golfer is a woman, there is not enough information to determine if the booing is related to sex or gender.

8. A: When teammates get along, it is easier for them to accomplish team goals (e.g., scoring, winning). Teammates that do not get along impede team success. Strategies that help build teamwork include designing small goals that the team can accomplish together and gradually increasing these tasks. Trust activities also help foster teamwork. The coach should also communicate to players team changes and the rationale behind those changes to diffuse any animosity between players. Teamwork does have transfer applications to other life events and situations, but it is not required for success.

9. B: Students in grades K-2 should be able to demonstrate progress toward more complexity in manipulative motor skills (c). Students in grades 3-5 should be able to refine and apply complex manipulative skills in the context of lead-up games (a). Students in grades 6-8 should be able to apply basic and advanced manipulative skills to sports, dance, and gymnastics, individually and on teams (d). Students in grades 9-12 should be able to create their own advanced movement skills and use them (b).

10. A: Hopping is defined as jumping off and landing on a surface using the same foot. It is classified as a locomotor skill because it involves movement between or among points in space. Bending (b), twisting (c), and turning (d) are all classified as non-locomotor skills because they involve body movements without changing position, and little or no movement of the body's support base.

11. B: Striking and kicking best illustrate manipulative skills as the body is moving with or controlling an object. Manipulative skills are more challenging and generally taught last because they combine locomotor and non-locomotor movements. Jumping (A), running, and jogging (C) are locomotor movements. Locomotor movements can be performed with a manipulated object but are locomotor movements when performed independently. Bending and twisting movements (D) are non-locomotor skills that can also be performed separately or with a manipulated object.

12. C: Catching is a manipulative skill that is classified as receptive, i.e., the catcher *receives* a moving ball or other object that another player has thrown, kicked, or stricken. Kicking (a), striking (b), and throwing (d) are all manipulative skills classified as propulsive, i.e., a player *propels* the ball or other object to make it move through the air, across a surface, etc.

13. D: The student lacks buoyancy and can fill up their lungs with air to help keep them afloat. Emptying the air in the lungs will decrease buoyancy and cause the student to sink. Drag slows down a swimmer and can be caused by wearing clothes or when the body is not in a streamlined position.

14. A: A muscular endurance goal requires that the muscle work for longer periods of time. Therefore, the higher the rep count, the greater the endurance. Increased soreness likely indicates that the overload principle was employed without progression to meet strength goals. Maintaining the same rep count over time does not indicate improvement effectiveness but simply maintenance. Maintenance is good for individuals who have met their fitness goals, but variation in activities ensures that the body continues to respond to exercise's physiological benefits. Increasing weight over time will gradually occur with endurance, whereas increasing weight complements a strength-building increase.

15. D: Weight training activities are effective in maintaining a healthy body composition, including weight loss as the body continues to burn calories hours and even days later. Cardiovascular activities, stretching, and Pilates are also effective, but the calorie burning occurs while engaged in the activity. It is best to incorporate various exercise modalities to have the greatest long-term impact for maintaining a healthy body composition.

16. A: Partner activities focus on relationships with others. While leading and following are partner activities, these are under the "relationship with others" movement concept. Partner activities are the normal progression before participating in larger team activities but are not movement concepts. High and low levels can also be taught in pairs but are subcomponents of the movement concept spatial awareness.

17. B: Force or effort is the most emphasized movement concept in the leap as it requires power on the take-off, and force is absorbed on the landing while maintaining body control. Rhythm is the movement concept that helps students develop creative movements to music or sounds, e.g., a drum beat. Time is the movement rate and is used across locomotor movements but is not the leap's dominant movement concept. The leap is performed at a medium or high level.

18. C: Manipulative skills are a combination of locomotor (traveling) and non-locomotor (bending) movements while using equipment (ball, hockey stick or puck, balance beam). Manipulative skills involve both gross motor and fine motor movements. For instance, when kicking and dribbling in soccer, tapping with the feet engages the fine motor muscles. During the kick, often conducted while walking or running (locomotor), the knee and waist bend (non-locomotor).

19. C: The three main categories of fundamental movement skills (FMS) are locomotor (A), manipulative, (A and, (B), and stability (D). Within the main category of stability are included the subcategories of rotation, (B) and (C), and balance, (C) and (D). Activities like spinning, twirling, rocking, bending, and turning demonstrate rotation. Balance can involve both stationary and movement activities. Both rotation and balance are components of stability. Locomotor skills involve activities like walking, running, and so on. Manipulative skills include activities like throwing, catching, hitting, batting, kicking, and transporting objects.

20. C: The Skill Themes approach focuses on teaching the fundamental movement skills (e.g., catching and throwing; running and sliding) required to perform more complex movements needed for sport and leisure activities. Sport Education is an approach to teaching team sports where every student has a role, such as player, coach, referee, or scorekeeper, which changes when starting a new "season" or the next sport. Teaching Games for Understanding (TGfU) is a tactical approach to teaching team sports that involves creating an environment where students have to make decisions during gameplay. Cooperative learning is a student-centered approach where students work together towards a common goal. Cooperative learning activities are evident or can be implemented in many curriculum approaches including the ones aforementioned.

21. A: Personal space is the focus of dancing freely in a contained area. General space is dancing freely around the gym or in an open space that belongs to no one or everyone. Varying spaces are different areas or types of space. For example, the teacher instructs half of the class to move in open space and restricts the other half to personal space movements. There can be an area for personal space activities and an area with general space activities or alternating between personal space (pause and bend) and general space (run). There are non-locomotor activities in personal space, but non-locomotor space is a fundamental movement skill and not a spatial awareness movement concept.

22. D: Having students play a game of catch would involve developing object control skills (the students would practice catching and throwing a ball) as well as locomotor skills (the students would likely have to run or walk as they try to catch the ball). Option A can be rejected because it does not directly develop object control or locomotor skills (though knowledge of shot put technique might be helpful in developing those skills). Option B can be rejected because it does not explicitly involve locomotor skills (running, jumping, walking, etc.), merely throwing (an object control skill). Option C can be rejected because it does not involve object control skills, just locomotor skills.

70

23. A: The teacher should consider the temperature and other weather conditions during long-term planning (e.g., yearly plan conducted at the end of the school year) before scheduling activities. For example, indoor activities (basketball, volleyball) should be scheduled indoors during extreme cold or hot temperatures, and outdoor activities (soccer, Ultimate Frisbee, track and field) should be scheduled during milder temperatures.

24. C: When Cooper and Potts developed and named aerobics in the late 1960s, it originally focused on the ability of the heart and lungs to use oxygen in sustained physical activity. Cooper was the first to differentiate aerobic capacity from body flexibility (A) and muscular strength (B) and to notice that some people who were very flexible or very strong still did not have good endurance for running, biking, or swimming long distances. Although aerobics initially focused on cardiorespiratory endurance exclusively, today's aerobics classes combine all the elements of fitness (D), incorporating stretching for flexibility and strength training for the muscles along with movements that raise heart and breathing rates for cardiovascular fitness in their exercises.

25. B: Zigzag running or alternating diagonal patterns are common in dual and team sports. Transitions occur in dual and team sports, but it is the transition from offense to defense and vice versa with footwork patterns differing across sport types. Curve patterns are not common in dual and team sports. Some team sports have high-level movements like jumping in volleyball and basketball, but dual sports such as tennis and badminton, use mostly medium-level movements but not defensive running patterns.

26. D: The grapevine consists of a side step with one foot, followed by a step behind the lead foot (cross step), followed by a side step (lead foot), then tap and repeat in the opposite direction. The grapevine is an extension of the step touch. Dance steps are broken down into shorter sequences and performed at a slower pace with a gradual or progressive increase in tempo and sequences.

27. C: Jumping fast and landing softly illustrate the movement concept of effort, which includes time and force. Tempo is the speed and force needed to jump fast and requires more effort, while landing softly requires less effort. Strong and weak are cues or terms used for emphasis or to describe the movement concepts, but these terms are ambiguous (e.g., the bodybuilder was strong; the illness made her weak) and do not clearly convey the movement concept of effort.

28. A: Kimberly needs to hear or see the skill cue to "step with the opposite foot of your throwing arm" to remind her of the movements. Practice will only work if Kimberly is practicing the correct movements. Working with a partner may or may not work, as it depends on the skill level of the partner. While all students may not master every skill, cues to help students improve should continue.

29. A: The bowler should use a heavier ball for more power to knock down all of the pins. There is no need for the bowler to move left since the middle pin is struck consistently. Putting more spin on the ball would help the bowler achieve a strike if the pins were struck from the side rather than down the middle. The bowler will likely lose power if the ball is thrown from farther away.

30. B: Lena should bend at the knees to get under the ball before passing it. Swinging the arms speeds up the ball, and it may go into the net, over the net, or upward towards the ceiling. Lena is facing the net for the ball to go into the net. The libero is a defensive player that takes the majority of defensive passes used during competitive play—not when teaching defensive skills in physical education.

31. A: Teambuilding activities, including trust falls, are often incorporated before sports practice or at the beginning of a physical education course to foster teamwork. One has to depend on another to meet a goal (e.g., to not fall). Taking turns and rotating team captains can create a balance in opportunities to engage, but teamwork will not develop automatically without a common goal or objective. It is controversial when students pick their teams because low-skilled, overweight, and obese students who frequently get picked last and face embarrassment tend to develop negative feelings towards physical activity. It is recommended that teachers pick teams to balance ability and safety.

32. C: Excessive alcohol consumption and smoking tobacco both increase the risk of heart disease. Living a sedentary or inactive lifestyle also increases the risk of heart disease and has been associated with similar poor health outcomes as smoking. Alcohol consists of empty calories and can contribute to the risk of excessive weight gain, leading to obesity. Eating disorders like anorexia nervosa or bulimia are psychological conditions with significant body image dissatisfaction and irrational fears of becoming overweight or obese.

33. D: At Level 0, Irresponsibility (b), students may "put down" classmates, verbally intimidate them, interrupt others, and are unmotivated. At Level 1, Self-Control (a), students control themselves enough not to interfere with classmate participation and learning, but may not fully participate themselves. At Level 2, Involvement (c), students are involved actively in learning and open to trying new activities. At Level 3, Self-responsibility, students more responsible for their actions can work unsupervised. At Level 4, Caring (d), students extend responsibility through cooperation, concern, support, and help with or for classmates.

34. D: Researchers have found that when teachers used motivational strategies of supporting student autonomy (a), providing structure (b), and being involved (i.e., demonstrating interest and emotional support), their strategy use was predicted by teacher perceptions of student self-determination; teacher self-determination affected this prediction (c); and student perceptions of teacher motivational strategies and student satisfaction with their own competence and autonomy improved student self-determination. However, they found that teacher self-determination did NOT predict student self-determination (d).

35. A: When students learn new skills or improve existing skills, they tend to feel a sense of accomplishment, which can lead to improved self-esteem (higher regard of oneself). This is the best answer. Option B makes a true statement, but wonder at human athleticism is not as clearly linked to improved self-esteem as learning new skills or improving one's skills (a student might feel wonder at a person who is athletically gifted and feel inferior in comparison). Option C can be rejected because there is no clear connection between learning to take turns and improved self-esteem. Option D can be rejected because endorphins, which can be released in the course of exercise, make a person feel good in the sense of being in a good mood, rather than fostering the general condition of improved self-esteem.

36. C: Motivation competence is developed when students experience success in easier tasks that builds confidence to try more difficult tasks. Self-regulation is awareness of how one learns and acceptance of the responsibility for the learning. Emotional development is the ability to manage feelings and emotions to focus on learning. Autonomous development is when learners perform tasks easily or automatically, as they have mastered the skill and no longer have to think about it.

37. A: Student choice has been shown to increase student motivation as it empowers students to make their own decisions rather than the teacher directing instruction. Physical education models of choice include cooperative learning, adventure education, sport education, and Teaching Games for Understanding (TGfU). Direct instruction and traditional teaching approaches are teacher-driven and based on the teacher's decisions. Competitive instruction has been shown to motivate highly athletic students but de-motivate less athletic or competitive students.

38. C: Self-assessment allows students to take ownership of their learning and fosters intrinsic motivation to learn and engage in physical activities for a lifetime. Grades are extrinsic motivators and have less impact on learning and physical activity engagement. Fitness testing studies show that a large percentage of students dislike fitness testing. Self-assessment of fitness has been shown to be more effective than fitness testing. Ability tracking is what a teacher may do to plan for appropriate instruction, as same-ability grouping has shown the most effective in games and moderate to vigorous physical activity engagement.

39. D: Alcohol, cocaine, Prozac, and other substances temporarily can reduce inhibitions so that students who are usually shy or introverted behave more sociably around peers (A). When students see substance use as a solution to being socially awkward and unpopular, they repeat it, which can lead to addiction. Conversely, students who were normally extroverted often withdraw socially when they become addicted to substances (B). Students who normally demonstrate self-control often behave more impulsively under the influence of substances (C).

40. D: Several studies of how sports-based life skills programs affected youth development outcomes have found that these programs improved social responsibility (a) and goal setting (d) in adolescent participants, and improved positive thinking (b), problem solving (c), and goal setting (d) in 10- to 12-year-old participants. Hence goal setting (d) was an improvement common to both age groups.

Subtest III: Professional Foundations; Integration of Concepts

1. B: Skill circuit variation can aid in skill development and refinement to meet diverse learners or mixed-ability groups. All students can work on the same skills but are challenged according to their ability. For example, in a shooting circuit, beginner students can work on technique closer to the basketball goal, intermediate students can shoot mid-range, and advanced students can shoot at farther distances at the same circuit. While student choice has been shown to increase motivation, students may not necessarily choose tasks that match or improve their ability. Combining mixed-ability or pairing advanced and beginner students is appropriate in some settings, e.g., peer assessment, but advanced and beginner students can become frustrated, so progress may suffer at both ends of the ability continuum. Beginner students may also get injured by intermediate and advance students, especially during gameplay activities.

2. A: The student has medical clearance to engage in physical education, which includes physical activity engagement. The teacher should provide low-impact activities that do not involve jumping, which puts additional stress in the knee joints. Allowing the student to choose from a list of exercises without jumps is appropriate, but not from a generic list or range of exercises because they may not have the knowledge of exercises that promote or impede a full recovery.

3. A: The teacher could add a defender to challenge Kevin with dribbling and changing directions which provides him with an authentic learning task similar to gameplay. Dribbling with two basketballs can help improve ball-handling skills but is not an authentic task done in basketball. Because Kevin can already dribble while running and changing directions, dribbling around cones is unlikely to improve his gameplay skills. It is the teacher's responsibility to differentiate instruction according to the objective, and moving on to another skill can create an environment where Kevin appears to get special treatment and can disrupt lesson planning and curriculum design.

4. B: Discipline is important when engaging in recreational activities since there is no one to monitor activity, hold the individual accountable, or help maintain motivation as would occur under the direction of a teacher or coach. The rules for recreational activities should be researched before engagement. Goals vary among individuals, but this does not explain why discipline is important. Outcome goals, such as fun, fitness, and competition tend to be clear, and creating goals helps with motivation and discipline.

5. B: Muscular fitness activities (weight training, push-ups) help prevent bone density loss, or the point that bones become porous or have tiny holes, which increases the risk of falling and broken bones. Women are most at risk. Age is a big contributor, given the changes in hormones and lower rates of weight-bearing activities. Engaging in aerobic activities (e.g., jogging, swimming, cycling) increases aerobic capacity and reduces the risk of cardiovascular disease and some cancers.

6. A: The numerous benefits of physical activity engagement are why physical activity is promoted in physical education programs. Consistent physical activity engagement reduces the risk of heart disease and other health conditions and improves mental health outcomes. Physical activity reduces blood pressure. Sedentary activities and poor dietary intake increase blood pressure risks. Engaging in muscular fitness activities lead to muscle hypertrophy and prevents atrophy or the wasting of muscle. Endorphins or "happy hormones" are released during physical activity which is another benefit of physical activity.

7. D: Working together with the principal to develop an exercise program that benefits student learning by enhancing the environment is an example of using administrator support and collaboration. (A) is an example of collaborating with an English language arts (ELA) teacher by using a novel to study a sport for the physical education (PE) component and character development and relationships for the ELA component. (B) is also an example of how to collaborate with an ELA teacher by watching a movie, studying its dance movements for the PE component and its themes for the ELA component. (C) is an example of collaborating with a Family and Consumer Sciences teacher by combining nutrition with exercise—a very natural and valuable combination as good nutrition and physical activity interact and mutually support one another in healthy lifestyles.

8. A: The teacher should recommend that this student engages in interval training with heart rate tracking to challenge the student to increase intensity in short bouts, which has improved cardiovascular fitness similar to endurance activities. Teachers can use the heart rate to determine criteria for high and low intensities. A pedometer is good for tracking steps but not intensity, and this student has an intensity issue. Students should be taught about the benefits of cardiovascular health, but awareness alone is not sufficient and does not provide a goal for the student. Engaging in activity for longer periods of time may increase the intensity, but there is limited time in physical education classes, and higher intensities in short bouts are more realistic. Research has also shown that students in physical education courses prefer high-intensity interval activities over long endurance activities.

9. C: The ability to hear aids in learning and motor performance, whereas hearing impairment impedes or can slow down learning and motor performance. In dance, the sound of music serves as a cue, as it alerts the learner when to perform each step. The ability to hear verbal cues also aids motor skill performance because it serves as a reminder of the desired outcome. Dance steps are usually introduced without music to help students focus on the movements.

10. B: Experts report that aerobic exercise can both elevate and stabilize mood (a); improve both sleep quality and self-esteem (b); reduce anxiety, even if the exercise is for as little as five minutes (c); improve concentration, alertness, and overall cognitive function, AND reduce fatigue (d). They

74

recommend exercise not only for its physical benefits but also its mental fitness benefits, including reducing stress.

11. C: A physiological benefit of exercise is it lowers the release of cortisol–a stress hormone and increases the release of endorphins–happy hormones. These physiological responses promote psychological outcomes or benefits including improved mood, positive thoughts, and increased confidence. Confidence also results from seeing the physical changes the body goes through from engaging in exercise.

12. D: Small-sided games are modified versions of games that allow for more opportunities to respond. Instead of five vs. five basketball, implementing two vs. two or three vs. three games increases student opportunity to integrate manipulative skills. Choice is a strategy used to increase student motivation. Leading and following can be used for isolation skills but do not foster integration in game-like situations. Mirroring works best with locomotor and non-locomotor movements. Demonstrations are more useful for refinement and integration of manipulative skills.

13. C: Research studies find that motor skills, endurance, and strength training all modify the spinal reflexes according to the specific behaviors each task requires. New blood vessels are formed (A) through endurance training but not motor skills or strength training. Motor maps are reorganized (B) through motor skills training but not endurance or strength training. New synapses are generated (D) through motor skills and strength training but not endurance training.

14. C: Summation of forces refers to producing the maximum possible force from any movement using multiple muscles. Adding up the forces generated by each individual muscle yields the total force or summation of forces. Related to this, the order of use is that the largest body parts are slowest, and being stronger and hence the initiators of power, they move first; the smallest body parts are fastest, and being in charge of coordination and refinement, they move last. Thus, the largest, slowest parts do not move last (A), and the smallest, fastest parts do not move first (B). Therefore, (D) is also incorrect.

15. C: Fitbit devices can help physical education teachers to support and increase student motivation and also include a line of designer fashion accessories. They can be used for both controlling weight and monitoring sleep quality (A). Students can self-monitor their own progress using Fitbit devices; they also can use them to challenge and compete with friends (B). They are not just stand-alone progress trackers (D); they also sync wirelessly with mobile smartphones and tablets and with charts, graphs, and badges available online for documenting improvements and gaining insights about physical fitness.

16. B: The integrated model best describes this approach that includes teaching other content areas to help foster holistic understanding. Quidditch, a fictional game in the Harry Potter series, is a game that was later developed for real-life physical education based on this approach. The tactical approach is used in team sports to develop decision-making skills. The cooperative games approach allows students to make choices on solving problems collectively. The skills theme approach focuses on skill development to foster skill competence and skill transfer across games and activities.

17. A: Although some skills are harder to break down, in general, PE teachers should demonstrate a skill as whole-part-whole, i.e., demonstrate the whole skill first; then break it down and demonstrate its components; and then demonstrate it as a whole again, rather than only demonstrating the parts (b) or only the whole (c). They should also give fewer, not more, cues (d), e.g., 1-3 at a time, according to student developmental levels and skill complexity.

18. A: A chasse is a ballet step adopted in jazz and modern dance and is similar to the gallop where one foot leads and the other follows. An axel is a turn used in jazz and modern dance but consists of turning while hopping. The ball change is a transition step used in jazz that consists of transferring weight on the balls of the feet, similar to the weight transfer that occurs in the grapevine step. The drop is an intentional fall to the ground, often after performing a leap.

19. A: Fifth-graders show ability to perform more complex movement skills integrating locomotor, non-locomotor, and stability movements by demonstrating mature motor patterns on obstacle courses and other increasingly complex settings. Playing simple games requiring manipulative skills (b) shows ability to manipulate objects using skills for sports lead-up activities and games. Describing important parts of throwing overhand (c) shows ability to describe and demonstrate elements of mature movement patterns. Understanding that practicing improves performance (d) shows ability to identify how to refine movement skills using movement concepts.

20. B: Resistance skills against peer pressure to engage in risky behaviors exemplify social and psychological life skills that PE promotes, according to the President's Council on Physical Fitness and Sports, which also identifies improved developmental outcomes from PE including motivation, self-confidence (a), self-regulation (c), and perseverance (d).

21. C: Negligence has occurred as the teacher did not ensure a safe environment by cleaning the spill. While not intentional, the teacher may be held liable. Accountability (A) is holding the teacher to certain standards. There may be a consequence for the incident. The circumstance may also be considered an accident where the teacher can be given a reminder to check the floors throughout instruction, especially after water breaks. Misfeasance (B) is a type of negligence that occurs when a teacher incorrectly implements a policy or practice. Malfeasance (D) is an act where the teacher intentionally breaks the law.

22. C: The National Board for Professional Teaching Standards (NBPTS) include creating an environment of respect and rapport with students. The board provides an example for addressing student problem behaviors of having the misbehaving student describe his or her behavior, state what made it disruptive, and identify solutions for the problem. This standard's example does not advise for the teacher to do these things (A): The student must do them for ownership, responsibility, and understanding of his or her behavior. Neither should the teacher ask a classmate (B) to do them for the same reasons. The standard does not recommend giving concrete consequences and solutions instead of discussing the problem (D).

23. A: The physical education standards are initially developed by SHAPE America, the largest national physical education organization that sets the standards for K-12 physical education and the Physical Education Teacher Education program (PETE). The state government and state-level physical education organizations adopt and can revise the national standards, which are then disseminated to the state's school districts. School districts and physical education teachers may have their own goals, but their practices must conform to the state requirements.

24. D: ESSA, or the Every Student Succeeds Act, recognizes the value that health and physical education have on developing the whole child. Parents should also be informed that physical education is not just fun and games but a way of learning psychomotor, cognitive, affective, and social domains. Title IX is the law that guarantees equal educational and athletic access to all genders. SHAPE America's toolkit is a resource that teachers can use in their instructional planning. IDEA is the Individuals with Disabilities Education Act that guarantees a quality educational experience for students with disabilities.

25. C: The teacher should keep quiet to maintain the student's trust. It is also not the teacher's responsibility to tell students' sexualities, regardless of where they land on the sexuality continuum. Contacting the student's parents could put the student in harm's way if the parents are not accepting. Unless there is evidence of the student harming themselves, there is no need to contact the school counselor. Contacting the counselor for LGBTQ resources is appropriate; however, the student's identity should remain confidential. Only the student should be allowed to decide if or when to come out. Therefore, the teacher should refrain from encouraging the student to do so.

26. B: Advocates can share this fact sheet with stakeholders and decision makers to show school health and physical education's importance and benefits to all students; use the guidance document (a) identifying necessary PE program elements to inform schools' structuring of PE programs; the position statement (c) to argue against cutting or reducing, and for expanding, maintaining, or funding PE because school, district, and state requirements for PE are the same as for other academic subjects; and the journal articles (d) to get practical advocacy advice and examples of advocacy challenges and successes.

27. B: The teacher breached duty or teacher responsibilities that includes maintaining a safe environment for all students. The teacher put this student's health and potentially life at risk. Assumption of risk is a defense against negligence and is when the student or participant agrees to engage in an activity that has an element of risk, such as in the extreme example of sky diving. Since students do not choose the activities done in most physical education classes, the assumption of risk defense is unlikely to be used in physical education cases. Proximate cause is another defense against negligence and suggests that accidents and injury would transpire with or without the teacher's presence. For damages to be awarded to the student or his family, he would have had to sustain injury, fatality, or suffer emotional harm.

28. D: Informing parents of the physical benefits of dance, careers in dance, and perhaps male role models in dance may help change their perceptions (stereotypes) that boys/males do not or should not engage in dance. Discussing the risks of playing football could be a strategy, but the parents may find this offensive because they are pro-football and may see the benefits as outweighing the risks. Suggesting that the student participate in both does not necessarily support the student because he does may want to play football. Telling parents that they are wrong will likely be offensive and negatively impact the teacher-parent relationship.

29. A: Typically, schools require students and their parents or guardians to sign the Agreement to Participate form, to acknowledge student and parent awareness of the inherent risks of participating in PE activities, and to confirm student agreement to participate and comply with safety regulations for all activities. K-12 schools do not limit signatories to only parents (b) or only students (c), and do not require PE teachers to sign (d).

30. D: This physical program meets proposed guidelines in student engagement and the large teaching area. SHAPE America recommends that students are engaged in activity at least 50% of the time. The equipment ratio and class size are ineffective characteristics of a physical education program. Class size recommendations are between 25 and 35 students with a 2:1 student-to-equipment ratio.

31. D: "The student will skip using a mature pattern" is an example of a SHAPE America grade level outcome for students in grade 1, as it is explicit about what students are expected to do, while "the student will demonstrate motor skills" is a SHAPE America standard that is broad or general.

Students will also apply movement concepts and it is hoped that students recognize value in physical activity, but these too are general standards rather than explicit outcomes.

32. B: The Society for Health and Physical Educators (SHAPE) America sets the national K-12 and physical education teacher education standards and each state-level SHAPE equivalent adopts these standards. Council for the Accreditation of Educator Preparation (CAEP) is responsible for accreditation of physical education teacher education programs and working closely with SHAPE America that also sets the health and physical education standards for teacher education programs. HPE is the acronym for health and physical education used in some programs. The Every Student Succeeds Act (ESSA) is a law designed to ensure equal opportunities for all students, including health and physical education.

33. C: For these students, achieving fitness through team sports is a more realistic goal. The teacher can employ competitive or team fitness activities where the focus is on a team goal rather than health, the standards, or body composition. Obese students tend to dislike physical education and physical activities due to bodies on display and the promotion of thinness or normal weight body mass indices, which are more pronounced during fitness activities. The teacher can provide instruction that promotes health and use the standards in a team-based approach, but doing so during traditional fitness activities may ostracize student engagement, especially when focusing on body composition.

34. A: Researchers have found that smaller class sizes and student–teacher ratios correlate with larger quantities of activity time, activity level, safety, and learning for students, whereas larger class sizes and student–teacher ratios correlate with smaller quantities of student activity times, levels, safety, and learning—that is, an inverse correlation. Studies show that students receive more and better physical education (PE) from teachers who teach only PE rather than dividing their teaching time and attention between PE and other subjects (B). Researchers are coming to increasing consensus that standards-based PE curriculum results in greater student physical activity (C). Well-maintained, safe, appropriate, and aesthetically appealing PE facilities and equipment also are found to increase and improve student activity (D).

35. C: Mr. Green can reduce the time it takes for attendance by taking it when students are engaged in an activity like the warm-up or instant activity. Setting an attendance time-limit will not likely decrease the time as 40 students need to be accounted for. Mr. Green could practice but practicing a managerial tool takes away from planning for instruction/learning. Squad lines where students sit or stand in the same spot make it easier to see absent students but unless a warm-up or activity is conducted in the squad lines, students have to wait to be engaged in activities.

36. A: The first step in the volleyball activity is for students to assume rotational positions, that is, with one setter in front and one in the back row, without overlapping. The second step is for a student to serve the ball. In the third step, following the serve, students move from their rotational positions to their base positions. The fourth step is for players to defend against attack by watching, calling, and passing the ball.

37. B: The best professional development not only improves a teacher's own expertise (A) and that of the teacher's colleagues (C) but both mutually as well as enabling physical education teachers to promote their own discipline. It enables teachers to improve instruction not only at the classroom level (D) but also at schoolwide and districtwide levels.

38. A: FITT = Frequency, Intensity, Time, Type. How long to work out (a) = Time, which is determined by the Intensity and Type of exercise. How to ensure overload without overtraining (b), burnout, or injury = Intensity. How often to work out to ensure enough stress to make the body adapt plus allow healing through enough rest (c) = Frequency. Specific exercises to do, and whether the workout is cardio, resistance (weight), or both combined (d) = Type.

39. C: Depending on state law, the teacher may be required to file a report personally or to a designated reporter for the school. In all cases, a person who is considered a mandatory reporter must make a report to the proper authorities any time they suspect abuse, neglect, or exploitation. Contacting the child's mother without proper training may put the mother at risk of abuse or furthering the child's abuse if the mother is complicit or a participant. Taking photos of the child is invasive and may cause further or undue trauma. As such, this is not a step that should be taken.

40. A: The Institute of Medicine recommendation is for children to spend an hour a day in moderate to vigorous physical activity (MVPA). But studies show that, in actual schools, physical education (PE) classes last about 23 minutes a day, with only 10 of those minutes spent in MVPA. In other words, children get about one-sixth the MVPA that is recommended from school PE classes. Researchers conclude that not only must children be physically active outside of PE classes, but also schools must increase how much children are active during PE class times.

Thank You

We at Mometrix would like to extend our heartfelt thanks to you, our friend and patron, for allowing us to play a part in your journey. It is a privilege to serve people from all walks of life who are unified in their commitment to building the best future they can for themselves.

The preparation you devote to these important testing milestones may be the most valuable educational opportunity you have for making a real difference in your life. We encourage you to put your heart into it—that feeling of succeeding, overcoming, and yes, conquering will be well worth the hours you've invested.

We want to hear your story, your struggles and your successes, and if you see any opportunities for us to improve our materials so we can help others even more effectively in the future, please share that with us as well. **The team at Mometrix would be absolutely thrilled to hear from you!** So please, send us an email (support@mometrix.com) and let's stay in touch.

If you feel as though you need additional help, please check out the other resources we offer:

Study Guide: http://mometrixstudyguides.com/CSET

Flashcards: http://mometrixflashcards.com/CSET